Published by:

Copyright © 2013 by Jacqueline Ripstein.
Published by 7 Colors LLC

Library of Congress Cataloging-in-Publication Data Ripstein, Jacqueline.
2014900189

ISBN # 978-0-9893804-2-3 Paper Book

**The Art of HealingArt...The Keys to Power and Awareness ©
Revised Edition Black & White
This Book is also available as a *Collector's Color Edition* (flexibound)**

This book connects you to the essence of knowledge. Each lesson is a step to your awakening, a compilation of wisdom to support you to live your most empowered, fulfilled, abundant, and optimum life.

x x x x x x x

**All Art is by International Fine Art Artist /Author
Jacqueline Ripstein ©**

**Cover Art: The Architect of his Own Destiny ©
By Jacqueline Ripstein (1983)**

Book designed by: Jacqueline Ripstein

Graphic Design: pixeldesignmiami.com

www.TheArtofHealingArt.com
www.jacquelineripstein.com
info@jaquelineripstein.com

The Art of HealingArt
The Keys to Power & Awareness

Jacqueline R Ripstein

JNDEX

Book: The Art of HealingArt...The Keys to Power & Awareness

The purpose of art, according to Aristotle, "is to represent not the outward appearance of things, but their inward significance." Jacqueline Ripstein's magical images bring forth the invisible realm and inspire us to experience a connection with higher levels of consciousness. Goethe wrote that the true work of art is "The mediator of the inexpressible." Jacqueline embodies this mediation in her art and in her persona. She expresses her vision of the angelic world in a unique, authentic and exquisitely beautiful way. How is she able to do this? She is, herself, an angel of art.

I met Jacqueline ten years ago while I was conducting research on the inward significance of the paintings of Leonardo da Vinci for my book: Da Vinci Decoded: Discovering the Spiritual Secrets of Leonardo's Seven Principles. I spent a week at her studio surrounded by her magnificent paintings and images from many different illustrated books about Leonardo. As I reached for one of the books, with the intention of leafing through it to find a particular passage from the Maestro's Treatise on Painting, I said to Jacqueline, " What we are doing would make Leonardo smile." The moment the words left my mouth we both saw the heading of the page I had randomly opened, which read "The Smile of Leonardo." I'm sure that Leonardo is smiling on the release of Jacqueline's book. In the beginning of his Treatise Leonardo penned a dedication: "May God, light of all things, design to enlighten me, who here treat of light." Jacqueline's dedication is manifest in the way she treats us to her enlightening reflections of Divine light.

Michael J. Gelb
Author of: How to Think Like Leonardo da Vinci

To adequately critique the profoundness of Jacqueline Ripstein's art requires a bold analysis of paintings.

She has demonstrated the skill of the Masters in a refined representation of real things, and the human form and face with expressions of the reactions to the physical world and transactions with people. She clarifies realism.

She has demonstrated the lofty skill of the Impressionists to soften and mystify reality that takes us to etheric levels of consciousness with a more mellow emotional flavor.

She successfully uses all colors and intensities to excite us from warmth to passion as she masterfully displays the path of now to that of the future.

Jacqueline Ripstein's paintings cover a broad spectrum from material consciousness to the etheric and the divine. These are the stimulus to enlighten mind and encourage physical health. To me her versatility and skills represent a frontier direction of art. Her leadership should foster a new school of painting which I title "Etheric Surrealism".

But most of all I believe her artistic representations are a grounding light for our evolution, from the chaos of our universe, which will help us to the peace of wisdom. Therefore I truly hope that her paintings will be displayed in every home and office of our land, as we remember that visual perception is more powerful and enduring than the written word. Her messages carry pervading wisdom.

Rev. Dra. Valerie V. Hunt
Professor Emeritus UCLA, Author, Scientist, Philosopher, Visionary
Is a scientist, author, lecturer and Professor Emeritus of Physiological Science at the University of California, Los Angeles."During her long teaching career she authored 6 books and 25 research articles. Scientifically she proves the existence of the human energy fields with broad degrees in Biology, Physiological Psychology, Science Education and Physical Therapy she taught frontier courses in twenty medical colleges and universities here and abroad."

*I*n Jacqueline's work we see humanity being nourished by crystal-line waters flowing from mystic realms of Being. In our current times of environmental and planetary change, we can draw inspiration from the image of our precious Earth being nurtured by the cosmic forces that sustain organic life. Here inner-dimensional truths are often symbolized in legends such as 'the Birth of New Being' in which celestial realms enter the earth through the font of sacred rivers of Light. Drawing from these archetypal myths and images, we discover in the paintings that the East and the West meet together in splendor where the Divine Father-Mother of the West and Brahma-Shiva's of the East pour forth the pranic or life force energies of the Divine Family that revitalizes the Earth.

Jacqueline Ripstein is, in essence, is one of the divine messengers whose visual screen is able to bring forth a scintillating field of ideographic language, a Rosetta picture that emanates a sense of transformation. Her ability is to draw upon effulgent realities from the past and future express the underlying unity of the consciousness that permeates all realms of Being.

Testimony (c) Dr. J.J. Hurtak, Ph.D.
President of the Academy for Future Science

" *J*acqueline has discovered the logic within the Harmonic Oscillators that allows the decoding of all information that flows from the Universe into us through our senses. Our perception expands. When we contemplate Jacqueline's Art, it may seem as if time stops."

Rafael Lopez Guerrero
President & Founder of FET (Foundatión EticoTaku for Innovation.)

" *T*he art of Jacqueline Ripstein fills a gap in the heart and heals from realms beyond by helping us to be more in touch with our inner-self. The messages hidden within Jacqueline's art resonate profoundly within the soul and awaken us to an invisible world. During moments of pain and loss, her art has a way to help heal. The invisible technique used by Jacqueline captures the viewers soul."

Jeffrey A. Wands
Author of The Psychic in you, Knock and AnotherDoor will open.

The Art of Jacqueline Ripstein is a powerful tool to see the future there is no progress in the future, if we don't learn from the past.

The painting "Confusion" (1982), by Jacqueline depicts the mess that our world is in today, collapsing slowly, as the Roman Empire did.

If we are not careful and watch every step we take, caring for our world, the consequences could be spiraling down into more "confusion".

I highly recommend you to take this spiritual journey with a highly gifted artist Jacqueline Ripstein, who expresses her inner feelings and relationship with the world through her art.

Her soul is reflected in her work..

Her book *The Art of HealingArt* and her art, can help raise our level of consciousness, helping us to uplift our world to higher planes of vibrations.

Iris Saltzman
Astrologer, Medical Intuitive and Parapsychologist.

*J*acqueline Ripstein's Art explores diverse themes: esoteric, philosophical and energetic, that shows to us the difference between the nature of rational intelligence and sensorial intelligence; containing her Art the four "elements," illuminated by her Light, a guideline to the true path of humanity, that flows within the Universe.

Jacqueline trespasses with her dynamic brushstrokes the barriers between the animated and the inanimate. It is here where she reaches the fifth element "ethereal"...where the essence of Love is transformed into form.

Since I met her, I knew she was pre-destined to alter the ways of Art expression, being this an inborn role of her essence, within every one of her paintings an ascended Master is hidden, with an Eternal message, that invites our senses to experience a true sensorial experience.

One day Michael Angelo was asked how he sculpted the stone, he answered; --"I do it in such a way that I recover the being trapped within it."-

A true artist goes beyond the appearance , rescueing the essence that lives within all form, trespassing dimensions only accessible for all those that know that the visible is only the tip of the iceberg, the place where all life originates.

In the multiple times we have talked, the magic of the "ethereal" has always been present,...the materialization, the messages are the essence of direct encounter of higher forces and guides of a higher destiny. I knew that behind her Art, there is a life's mission that involves all of us in an alive Cosmic Chess, the same painting she did years ago,(1992) being this masterpiece an alive sample of the essence becoming alive.

Jacqueline utilizes the Light as a vehicle to unite Heaven and Earth.

"Light is the shadow of God"...Einstein.

Jacqueline has been called to be a "Master of Masters", creating a New Art School, where the Arts, energy and Light will be the medicine of the Soul, that will help ascend the Human Frequency.

Lourdes Méndez
Consciential Antropologist, Researcher and Interpreter of the Universes Symbols. Astrologer.

Prologue

We are all students in the School of Life...

I have used the term *"lesson"* in the title of each chapter of this transformational book because each chapter expresses an apprenticeship in the journey of Life. Each individual who crosses our lives is a teacher. Teachers in the school of Life are not only those who love us, but also those who have hurt us, or those who have created deep pain within us. These teachers help us grow and discover our weaknesses, ego, fears, and insecurities. As we realize who we are, we encounter our real potential for increased inner strength; we discover our Glory, our Light.

A lesson is an occurrence that serves to teach us something; it can encourage us to grow up. Each lesson in this book reveals a specific key to our growth. Upon viewing the images and messages in each one, readers will recognize feelings of pain, anger, hatred, and low vibrational energies that have kept them anchored in their past. This recognition represents a unique opening moment that helps us unburden the pain we carry, as we free ourselves from the lowest emotions that drag us down. Images and words can trigger *remembrance,* in which a sudden flash of understanding appears, creating an "aha" moment that reveals the knowledge that is stored within our souls. This book is a wake-up call, a motivational instrument for an awakening humanity.

The lessons in this book are inspirational conduits of knowledge to help us expand our consciousness. Recognition of Love, Forgiveness, and Compassion raises us to higher states of mind where we regain the connection to the Divine being within us all, uniting our Light with the Creator.

Garden of the Prophets © 1982 Jaqueline Ripstein

The Art in this book is a mirror reflection of Our Souls.
The Supreme lesson of Life is Love.

With every step we take, every thought we have, we are
nourishing the shadows – or nourishing the Light.

I dedicate this book to God, to you, to our children, and
to their children, to all humanity.

May the Light be our guide.

To my daughters, Stephanie and Arlette, to my
son-in-law Jose, to my grandchildren Moises, Sara,
Alan and Daniel, who I adore.
To my dear parents, my brother and sister, my family, and
loving friends, to my collaborators, to my beloved pets...
Thank you for sharing this lifetime with me. I love you.

To my Teachers.

Introduction

Only those who see the Invisible, can do the Impossible.

Bibbidi-Bobbidi-Boo! I used to sing this and dance to it when I was four years old. My father had given me the most wondrous magic wand made from cardboard and wrapped in aluminum foil. It sparkled like a star! I believed in magic – my wand and my paintbrush transported me to the Invisible World. I lived then, and still live now, with wonder and excitement. Life for me has been a magical journey.

Art has long been both an inner need and something that has led me to growth and fulfillment in my life. Before I start to paint, as an act of reverence I always light a candle and pray to be guided by the Divine.

This book's purpose is to reveal the hidden messages through art, to reveal the Light of God within all of us and the Invisible dimensions that create our everyday lives. May it serve to guide you in an inspirational journey to where the art and its messages become a guide to reveal your Inner Light being. Let each painting be the Mirror of your Soul.

Eternal Love © 1987 Jaqueline Ripstein

I could never have imagined that during my artistic career a mystical journey would unfold before my eyes. That I would work with certain unseen and higher dimensions of energy and colors, encountering beings that vibrated within the Light or within the darkness, was beyond my wildest dreams. Visibility, after all, depends on the eyes of the observer and the instruments used. What we physically observe is very limited, which of course limits us in viewing the vastness of Creation. Thus, feelings, thoughts, and emotions may also be classified as existing within the "Invisible" fields.

My goal in revealing these unseen dimensions is to offer a breath of hope to our humanity by showing from where we create our lives, as the inner Light beings that we truly are.

In order to manifest the law of attraction we need to understand first from where we create it all. Every second we are manifesting our lives, not from the "visible, material planes," but from within our subtle realms, from our invisible dimensions that connect us to the Eternal Flow of Creation. Our feelings are creating thoughts, our thoughts create actions, and our actions manifest a matching reality in our actual, physical, everyday lives.

In 1977, after a few years of showing my art, my friend Flor Siqueiros invited me to exhibit my paintings in the Government City Library of Cuernavaca, Mexico. Midway through the show, the wife of the then-governor called and invited me, to my great surprise, to receive a distinction diploma. Upon my arrival, she gave me close to one hundred sheets of paper on which children and adults alike had jotted down the messages they had perceived as they viewed my paintings at the exhibition. As I read them, tears came to my eyes. I realized they had discovered something I'd never thought about: My art was a wide-open portal for messages that nurtured emotions in a positive way and boosted energy. At that very "aha!" moment, I realized that my paintings had a life of their own and I, like my brush, was merely an instrument of the Light of our Creator. Very clearly, I realized my life's mission. I was being guided to be a tool, a messenger, not the message. I realized my art was a doorway, a portal to Invisible realms, connected to emotional healing and spiritual power. Each work of art became a conduit that opened and revealed specific new paths to knowledge and lessons of life. What's more, I understood that others too could achieve through each painting an energetic connection with higher levels of their consciousness.

I learned about life's *chiaroscuro*, a word that refers to the optimum balances between light and shadow. In art it is an essential tool that we use to enhance the delineation of character and to obtain a more dramatic effect. In order to reveal the Light of God within each painting, I had to learn to use extreme contrasts of light and shade. The stronger the darkness I painted, the more I could show the rays of the Light of God, a revelation that led me to understand the sense of our individual existence and the contrast between our Light and the many shades of shadows that hide within us. The stronger my tests of life were, the higher the opportunity to reveal the Light I was given. We can never dissolve these shadows; we can maneuver them to our benefit, to reveal our weaknesses -- the areas that we have to work on -- to reveal our Light. This is an essential task to discover *the chiaroscuro of life. When we remove our weaknesses, the Light within us emerges.*

The main goal in our lives is to own what is within us, as we identify and accept both our Light and our shadows. Only then can we master our lives. Once we have that awareness, and have seen the order in our chiaroscuro design, we may use the shadows to reveal our Light.

Seeing through our physical eyes is limited, while seeing through our Invisible eyes reveals the unlimited expressions of Life.

In my research for Invisible techniques, all kinds of trials appeared on my path. Being a pioneer in an unknown field is not an easy task. It takes countless hours of study, research, and experimentation. Many times I felt like giving up.

My search for the Invisible realms, as well as techniques to sate my great inner hunger to show through art the concealed Light within all of us, seemed an unreachable goal. But a force immeasurably stronger than I has fortified and encouraged me, giving me the strength to continue. My mystical artistic path has been full of surprises.

Through my art I have come to comprehend that when the great masters created their artwork, they did so in elevated moments of inspiration, connecting and transmitting high vibrations and information that was hidden within the Invisible World. Their art inspires us and enables us to recognize our own true spiritual path of Light and Love.

The Invisible World is the spiritual dimension where we create our thoughts and feelings that will, in turn, manifest as the corresponding experiences we encounter in our physical lives. The Invisible World manifests through the arts as the creative forces merge (use of the right brain) and elevated levels of inspiration flow. This state transports us to higher dimensions where we can tap into messages and events that may not yet have manifested and that are neither tangible nor visible. These revelations unveil the essence of our beings of Light and the true meaning of Life's secrets. All is created from the Invisible World.

The arts, created from the Soul, serve as conduits to help us access higher levels of consciousness. Doing so lifts and liberates our own creativity and inspirational levels. There are low-vibrational arts that are not created through the Spirit, but rather through the ego's darkness and its empire of shadows, fears, and low emotions. The effect of these vibrations on human beings is to bring them down and to depress them, feeding their need to suffer. The arts then become an escape from torment.

Humans often take drugs and alcohol to create a high, a way to duck out of darkness and experience "the Light." In reality, drug use is not a true high because the Light that one perceives is illusory, and the price of this action, and possible addiction, is too dear. True Light realization comes only through hard work on oneself.

When we appreciate such wonders as the Sistine Chapel, or listen to high-frequency spiritual music, such as that composed by Baroque musicians, Mozart and Bach, our entire being is lifted up, transported to a high state of scintillation. These magical moments of inspiration truly do elevate us, and suddenly we find ourselves in Heaven. The connection to our Spirit vibrates within us as the highest levels of consciousness fill our hearts. It is our great privilege to be living in new and higher vibrational times that are stimulating our creative forces while providing an opportunity for raising our consciousness.

Our present calling is to connect with our inner Self, our Spirit, Mother Earth, and all living beings that inhabit the earth, for we are one with all life and one with our Creator. Human beings are the continued expression of Mother Earth and of the cosmos. We play an essential role in the energetic links of life; we contain the inner power to rise above any lower-vibrational levels. To lift our consciousness from the earthly, physical plane is the key to our growth and expansion, the key to our Enlightenment.

Within us are the same elements that make up all creation: water, earth, fire, air, and ether. This composition unites us with all in existence, as we vibrate within a multiverse that is vibrating for eternity. *Life is a dance of multiple energy vibrations.* We move within the planet, and the planet vibrates within other systems. For this reason, each person has the power to change and influence the whole in a positive way.

The Arts and the Invisible World are the connections that guide me to find those remote spaces that are hidden to the naked eye but which, nevertheless, create our truest reality. I thank God for giving me the free will to explore and choose the path of the Arts.

In the history of humankind, the Arts have played an essential role in depicting the inner life of human feelings, whether in thoughts, words, or actions, and their inextricable connection to the Divine. *The Arts are the silent language of the Soul.* The creative forces through all the Arts lift up our hearts, filling our lives with Love and inspiration; they elevate us as the right side of our brains awakens, rousing the slumbering artist within. Ascending is a process in which we learn to become ever lighter, finer, and increasingly subtle as we merge with our Spirit. There is no separation between body and Soul within high-vibrational levels of awareness.

During inspirational moments, we realize the transformation of our lives. In the time that a flash of lightning lasts -- one second -- we breathe in and lighten our load. We inspire and are inspired. The word "inspire" contains within it the union of body and spirit: in-spiritus. Inspiration ignites sudden lucidity in us, unleashing creative forces that open our lives to transformation. These "aha!" moments are openings of the highest inspirational impact. They help us expand, as we open doors to possibilities we never before imagined.

With my art, I have learned to reveal the Light through the darkness. Life is a constant game between these two forces. Darkness has several levels of shadows that vibrate at various frequencies; these are identified with diverse egos and low emotions. Low-frequency feelings pull us down, taking us by the hand into realms of darkness that are full of pain, anger, agitation, anxiety, guilt, doubt, and fear. As we descend, these low-energy emotions feed on themselves, and intensify. The more we use them, the more we crave them. Yet at some level, most of us realize that we are the victims of our own creations, and that in any fall, we have the opportunity to rise again. Toward this end, exposing the ego and its minions of darkness can be our best approach. It has the potential to reveal to us our own Light. It is the hard and continuous work of consciousness to keep these two forces in constant balance.

Anxiety, doubt, confusion, uncertainty, and fear by any other name can gut creativity and hinder awakening, while hope, faith, clarity, and kindness give us the key to ending all conflict and suffering.

The awareness that gives rise to all good qualities is not about destroying the ego, but rather lies in the understanding that darkness cannot be destroyed. If we learn to balance this force, to use its energy to reveal and share more Light, then our real powers will be unleashed. Colors are composed of the energetic union of radiance. *Awareness* is the highest vibratory force of Light Consciousness. Strength, valor, perseverance, faith, Love, and happiness are manifestations of White Light and high-vibrational colors. Black represents a lack of color, emptiness, fears, depression, darkness, hopelessness, unhappiness, low spirits devoid of all energy. It is the lack of Light.

In the process of our existence – and after overcoming the challenges of life – layers of egoic darkness melt away. To confront our darkness is a difficult task that takes courage, awareness, and desire for growth. This process is sort of like peeling an onion: the more we penetrate its interior, the more its layers adhere and get easily mixed up with its core. It becomes more difficult to remove them. We live in *maya*, or the state of *illusion*, and we are trapped in it easily. This state governs our lives, and it is in this trap where we have become lost, accepting our darkness rather than our Light. We are constantly bombarded by negativity – shows and news reports that dwell on crime, depravity, illness, disasters, and war. Sometimes there is even derision of human suffering, including the degradation that can make a joke of our lives. We are being motivated by an ego system which holds us completely in its thrall. Our Light can barely peek through.

We are more accustomed to pain than to joy, to darkness than to Light.

To discover our Essential Eternal Self and to learn to reveal it is a process of consciousness. Our Higher Self moves within us through our highest vibrations of energy; these higher-energy vibrations connect us through invisible fields to joy, Peace, and Love.

"A Picture's Meaning Can Express Ten Thousand Words." Chinese proverb.

In this book each lesson is learned through its works of art and their hidden messages. Each message is a step toward the revelation of our own truth, toward our Enlightenment. Each image captures different dimensions of reality, it contains a silent language that vibrates directly to our Soul, awakening in us states of inspiration and awareness. The book that you have right now in your hands radiates high, scintillating energies. Its purpose is to inspire, rouse, and motivate, to infuse our lives with joyous anticipation, to shower us with Light, and to lift us over any darkness that may be anchoring our lives – pain, anger, guilt, fears, resentment, sorrow, jealousy, grief, and low self-esteem. These are all negative energies, thoughts and feelings that limit us; they can be counted on to create physical pain and illnesses that have an emotional source. Depression, defeat, and fatigue represent lower feelings that are caused by our exhausted responses to the many obstacles and trials of life. They diminish our faith and deplete our joy of living...*our Light.*

Through depression and many other dark low emotions, our Light dims and our immune system declines along with it. White blood cells are the physical Light of our body.

Colors can be used to heal, restore and to uplift us.

Colors are vibrating light energies, each "color ray" produces a sound that affects matter. There are seven color rays, each represents a different spiritual force, that emanates from the white light. They are perpetually vibrating - at different frequencies. Color vibrations are a source of power, each one having a general as well as a specific function and purpose. Each Era represents another Ray, human beings incarnate under a particular ray and are influenced by other subordinate rays, we receive colors, and we emanate colors, until we sharpen our senses and awaken to higher states of consciousness, this vibrational language will remain a secret to us. We are entering Aquarius time, the correspondent ray to this Era is the violet ray known as the "seventh ray." The Invisible techniques I developed in my Art contain the violet flame power. *May this vibration descend as a beam of spiritual energy and burst into a spiritual flame in your heart, as its flame reveals within you the qualities of Love, Compassion, and Forgiveness.*

An increasing concern for the welfare of humankind, especially for our children and their future, has always been in my heart. My proposal for World Peace is to reunite humanity (regardless of differences of religion, race, culture, or ideology) by drawing on the common creative forces within all human beings and the Arts, which feed our Spirits with Peace and Love. Freeing us from any burden or attachment, they elevate us to higher states of consciousness in which we shine, while also reflecting that brightness and glory onto all of humanity. *Working within -- and as -- this One Creative Light, we are united.*

I have accepted my mission with respectful responsibility: to be a simple brush, through which art may reveal the invisible bridge between Heaven and Earth. It is my privilege and duty to help create a new world of *Peace and Love* as a legacy to all beings -- a new world, where our Spirits will flower in our everyday lives. The arts, prayer, and meditation are powerful and wide-open channels through which we may recognize and express our Inner Self, and in so doing, create World Peace.

My wish is that this book's inspirational messages and art will aid men and women to reunite with their Higher Selves, manifesting the Light of Our Creator through every action. Together, we can create harmony among all people, while respecting and restoring balance with Mother Earth and the Universe. May the Light of our Creator shine through our every thought, word, and deed, and may we leave a legacy to our children and their children as we give birth to a World of Peace and Love.

Man and the Cosmos © 1982 Jacqueline Ripstein

Lesson 1

Man and the Cosmos©

" As it is above, so it is below; as it is within, so it is without."
" The lips of wisdom are closed, except to the ears of understanding."
The Kybalion

The all is mind; the universe is mental.

**The great work of Creation has come to an end,
to return again to its beginnings.**

The rebirth of a humanity that holds higher awareness is in the dawn.

**This new humanity is glorious in its wholeness, its magnificence, beauty,
and wonder.**

**When each human being reflects brilliance unto another, a chain reaction
is created, and Light is ignited in all of Creation.**

God cannot be put into words because God transcends language.

The Creator is Eternal.

The culmination of Life occurs simultaneously at the highest levels of existence.

Where it is not day, where it is not night ...

Where no distinctions are made about color or gender ...

**Where the sun and the moon maintain a dance of Light, which flows with
the continuous movement of the Universe ...**

Separation disappears in the orgasmic union of all Creation.

The Zero Point is the nest of all Life.

The essence of the self is Purity, Glory, Freedom, and Light...

Man and the Cosmos © 1982 Jacqueline Ripstein

*I*n the Zero Point, everything has already been manifested. The past and the future are combined into one unique reality, the Present.

The Present exists within the invisibility of the Zero Point.

We are living in times of many changes, and a Spiritual shift is occurring now. To prepare us to be part of this shift is one of the goals for this book's guidance. In the school of life you're given a test that teaches you a lesson. Each lesson in this book has a purpose, each lesson prepares you for the next step of your awareness. Training your mind will help you see through the veils of the ego and its kingdom of darkness, as you learn to reveal and shine your Light.

The lesson within this painting will help us realize that a a Supreme Power governs the universe. This lesson contains the first step to our awakening. Wakefulness is the state of being conscious. To realize our connection to the various levels of human existence is an essential step to understanding the vastness of our magnificent essence. We are connected to the material dimension, from the smallest scale of the micro-cosmos to the expanded universal one...the macro-cosmos; from the visible material plane to the invisible where our Spirit shines.

As we learn to focus on who we are and what role we play in the Universe, we strive to see beyond the boundaries of this physical existence. The larger dimension cannot be seen; only a very small part of what exists in this universe can be seen by our physical senses. This larger dimension is what I call the Invisible World. All we see is illusory and a fragment of something greater. Life will not be fully understood until we recognize the Eternal Forces of Light within us.

We awaken step by step to our own reality by following the inner guidance of the *Universal Self*, which is the highest level of Consciousness of our being, pulsating within the heart that harbors the Light of Creation. As we learn to integrate ourselves with these higher-energy vibrations by becoming self-aware and practicing self-observation, we can access our inner dimension, where we become one with all living beings. Separation is the fundamental ego illusion that holds us in a dream state, fooling us into believing that the Spirit's reality is the dream. As we recognize our Truth and take full responsibility for our actions and their results, the universe conspires to bring us what we wish for the most.

We are drops within the same ocean, all united in this Ocean of Love. If a single human being suffers, that person's suffering affects us all, regardless of where on Earth he or she may be. If an animal suffers, its pain energy will radiate in all directions, bringing pain to human beings. Each being is an essential link in an energetic chain that unites all Creation. When we recognize and then realize these truths, we will possess the awareness necessary to rise to a higher state of Consciousness; we will develop Compassion.

Each individual who dwells in a constant state of suffering has an effect on the whole of humanity. We are sensitive antennas that are connected to the universe. Due to our busy schedules, stress, and distractions, we often do not perceive the subtle messages the universe is always trying to relay to us. We are like a radio that is trying to receive a transmission when it is turned off. The universe is still broadcasting its loving guidance, but we cannot receive it through our doubts, fears, and worries.

There are steps to climb as we awaken to our truth. The first one is to focus our attention within ourselves; we are then creating an "awareness state."

Among the steps to acquiring a new, more focused inner connection is awakening our curiosity. Searching and inquiring into our existence will transport us from the noisy, superficial, everyday living that constantly traps us to a deeper level of peace and equanimity, to the Eternal place within each of us, where we merge in oneness with the Light of our Creator.

Throughout my thirty-seven years as an artist, I have discovered that in moments of high inspiration, I am transported to invisible and rarified dimensions where all that exists has already been created. Since 1982 I have called this dimension *The Zero Point*. This is the space where all co-creation with the Universe happens, where through inspiration I perceive and see my artwork before I have physically created it. Many times, I am given the written message before I perceive the image. Sometimes I paint what I see in my vivid dreams. Each painting then becomes my teacher, as it reveals to me the specific energy it taps into, unveiling a lesson of life contained within that vibration. One thing is clear to me: I am not the one who creates; I am merely the instrument of the Creator.

To be creative, you've got to question continually and remain curious always.

My deep curiosity about who we really are and my inner need to portray through Art "the Light of God" within us are what prompted me to search beyond all visible art and all material means of expression. My studio became an alchemist's laboratory as my curiosity was ignited to go beyond what our eyes can see. My mystical art journey had begun. That is how I

---

(1) Rupert Sheldrake proposed the "hypothesis of formative causation," which emphasizes that memory is inherent in and pervading all of nature. From there, he began to build a theoretical system, which (assuming that there are invisible influences over the beings that inhabit Earth) culminates in a series of concepts such as "morphic fields," or "morphic resonance."

came to discover new Invisible techniques never before used in the Arts field, creating methods for transforming the viewer. My art became a living experience, triggering with its high vibrations and its surprise factor a perceptible change in us. For centuries artists have searched for and portrayed the importance of the Light of our Creator, but they were always limited by the boundaries of color materials that exist in the physical plane.

During the many years that I have been working with invisible dimensions, I have encountered multiple other dimensions of existence, as well as unique colors. They seem to have a Life of their own. Their vibrant hues and energy vibrations are not the same as the colors manifested within the limited color spectrum of what we can perceive with our physical eyes. They go beyond the five senses. They flow, vibrating within all of Creation. Constant messages are being delivered by the universe, messages that are ever guiding us to discover our Light. Color and music transmit more than we can see or hear within our own vibrational range; they are silent languages of the Spiritual World. Years later when I read about biologist Rupert Sheldrake's theory of *morphic fields*, (1). I understood and clearly confirmed my mystical and artistic experience. Each painting experience I encounter connects me to those dimensions in which all answers are being delivered constantly.

Creativity is a process through which we utilize the unique gift we all carry within us. It is the power and capacity to create beyond the limitations of the mind. Connected to our right brain, it is the language of our Soul. *I have learned that once I tap into the invisible realms, my control is over! I have to let go in order to receive the right guidance. This is how the natural abilities we are born with, connect us beyond our material reality. Our gift is God's gift, and our mission is to share it with humanity. We all are born with a gift, and as we uncover the heavy layers of the ego, the gift is activated within us.* As we learn to shift our physical personality, which is usually shadowed by the ego looming large, to the magnificence of our Spirit, or Higher Self Being, we co-create our lives and a world full of Love and Joy .

In *The Presence of the Past: Morphic Resonance and the Habits of Nature,* Sheldrake reclaims the holistic perception of psychology that asserts that human beings, besides being individuals, belong to a collectivity that each person would do well to embrace and know.

Thus, we can understand not only that invisible forces unite us and influence us, but that we vibrate and abide in multiple dimensions not perceived by the human senses. All these realities occur in the *Invisible World,* which parallels our physical, material, and visible realm. Everything that exists in this universe is energy, manifested from the most subtle realms of energetic structures to the densest realms of vibrating matter. In the material world this energy is condensed and trapped. It is all an illusion: we perceive material objects to be solid, and they are not. Science has taught us that all matter vibrates. The more it condenses, the slower its atoms vibrate.

How should we understand this? It is important to appreciate that we are far more than what we see and believe ourselves to be. We have more skills than we can begin to imagine. And we need to learn to use these capabilities with utmost humility and purity of intention to co-create a world of Light and Peace.

Have a look around you right now; take in your surroundings wherever you find yourself. Notice the colors of the objects and any movements or sounds. Now imagine there is much more than you can see. There is a dance of molecules and energy, discrete intelligences, and creative energy that is born at the Zero Point. This is the field that I call *The Invisible World*, and we'll be tapping into it more and more throughout this book. It is the awareness inside you of other dimensions and portals that will elevate you to the Spiritual Being that you really are.

Creativity is what connects us to *The Invisible World*. The illusion of separation within the material world makes us "perceive" separation, even though it is only that -- an illusion. The positive and negative energy forces, male and female, Yang and Ying, move in a constant dance of creation, a balance of Light and darkness that is the true manifestation of Light.

We are Beings who are made of energy, and we radiate extraordinary vibrations (colors and sounds) that identify each of us as unique. This vibratory force fluctuates according to our emotional states. Low emotions, like fear and depression, decrease our vibratory frequency. Love, Compassion, and Inspiration elevate us and place us in the Zero Point.

We are beings emanating energy of multiple colors and sounds of Light.

It is not that transformative changes are coming "someday." It is that we are already living in times of transformation. The long-awaited Age of Aquarius has arrived. The Zero Point is approaching, and we are preparing to enter a new dimension of the color violet and invisible ultraviolet colors. The Violet Flame is a unique Spiritual energy of self-transformation. A new dimension of higher vibrations and energy is dawning in which everything that is moving with a low vibration will be forced to upgrade. In order to do this, lessons and experiences will be manifested to invalidate the ego and its illusions of scarcity and superiority, thereby helping us to raise our own vibrations to higher levels of Consciousness. Creativity will flourish as a new Golden Era sparkles in. Our Spirit will be our guide.

The value of material things will steadily fade, forcing us to see beyond this physical dimension. Tests of Life will be our blessings, empowering us to wake up to the new reality as we consciously co-create the next stage of our evolution.

Losing all desire to harm another human Being or an animal is an essential part of our awakening. Although you, yourself are unlikely to take part in it, mass torture and killing happen every day on this planet. It affects us as well, regardless of how geographically far removed and consciously unaware of it we may be. Given that we are all connected, the work to stop anger, cruelty, and even indifference must start within ourselves. To develop a peaceful state within ourselves is essential, as we open to expansion in Consciousness. We should persevere in our efforts to master our lives and "kill" (meaning to gain control over) the ego. The ego promotes anger, war, and greed. In all wars, all people lose. The energy we use to hurt others, even if only to marginalize or look down on them, will always come back to us many times stronger. This is a law of the universe.

(2) Schumann resonances occur because the space between the surface of the Earth and the conductive ionosphere acts as a closed waveguide. The limited dimensions of the Earth cause this waveguide to act as a resonant cavity for electromagnetic waves in the ELF band. The cavity is naturally excited by electric currents in lightning. Schumann resonances are the principal background in the electromagnetic spectrum.

Earth's background base frequency, or "heartbeat," (called Schumann resonance, or SR) is rising dramatically. Though it varies among geographical regions, for decades the overall measurement was 7.8 cycles per second. This was once thought to be a constant; global military communications developed on this frequency. Recent reports set the rate at over 11 cycles, and climbing.

As we approach the Zero Point, time is accelerating every day. Our days of twenty-four hours are starting to feel shorter and shorter. For thousands of years, the Schumann Resonance (2) (a measure of the beating heart of Mother Earth) had a rate of 7.8 cycles per minute. Since 1980 it has been increasing, and today it is at around 12 cycles.

As what we once knew becomes increasingly less relevant, we can no longer presume to make "forecasts." We have stepped off the comfortable terra firma of what we assumed our lives were about on the outside and are delving into the Mystery on the inside. This is a time to let go of all our "shoulds" in order to take action and reshape our Life in truth, goodness, and beauty. Parental and societal ideas about your Life schedule and your status are much less important now. It is time to let them go. The laws of Mother Nature are changing. Our physical bodies are trying to adapt to the changes. Societies are also experiencing the changes. People are rebelling. The material world is imploding from within. Old illusions are vanishing before our eyes, ushering in an Age of Enlightenment. ***The Awakening has begun.***

For centuries we have walked together in myriad civilizations as One Humanity and as individuals. We have laughed joyfully and cried wretchedly. We have fallen and risen together – always together. Now, I invite you to be present in your lives, to create and participate in this moment of great changes. The time for manifesting the limitless grandeur that you were created for is now. We are evolving and awakening to new opportunities for self-discovery.

These changes are also affecting our bodies in very noticeable ways. Maybe you feel more tired than before, or find yourself eating differently, or wake up in the middle of the night wanting to go for a run. Have you thought about changing your career? How about becoming the artist you would love to be? You may feel that there is not enough time to finish your tasks. All this is OK. It's your body's and inner Being's way of dealing with the new higher-energy vibrations. United, the journey will be easier.

This is our time to awaken – to co-create a world that is healthy, peaceful, and prosperous for all. Realizing our Oneness, we are being reborn.

Our Being of Light is preparing itself. The uterus of Mother Earth, too is ready for the birth of the New Age. A new humanity, a new planet Earth is being born now.

In winter everything seems to die. Life becomes dormant to prepare for rebirth. Spring returns, the sun shines again, and new energy is unleashed. This is what is happening now. Such are the changes that humanity is experiencing. The opportunity is arising for us to finally awaken from our long winter's nap. ***Together we can fall again or rise to our true Light.***

Reflections

Life is a present when we become conscious of it. To live awakened is the present of our Present.

This lesson contains the first step to our awakening. As we learn to focus in on who we are and what role we play in the Universe, we strive to see beyond the boundaries of this physical existence. It is a quest propelling us to focus our attention within, to see within our Invisible World, to expand and stimulate our curiosity. We embrace a new life of conscious living.

The Zero Point is the dimension wherein all of Creation overflows with rich and meaningful possibilities. Life's great abundance flows all the time through you, offering limitless potential. All this happens in the Present moment. Take the opportunity – *carpe diem* (seize the day)! It is yours to embrace.

When the sun's strength is reflected, when the moon's glow is activated, when the Divine Spirit sparkles as it merges with the body, when the masculine embraces the feminine, when Heaven comes down and Earth rises to enfold it, it is in that second within the Present moment that the portal opens and welcomes us into the Zero Point. This is the dimension where all has been created. It is the nest of Divine Love wherein we are nurtured and embraced, and where all of Creation swirls and swoons within the Divine Light of the Creator.

In the Zero Point, there is no night and there is no day. There is no particular identity. There is no male, no female. All is contained in *Oneness.*

The Yang balances with the Yin. It is the space where all Creation manifests, where the Whole is merged with the Eternal Light. Therein lies the Essence of Eternal Life. The Present is here and now. At this very second, all is available for you to enjoy, to experience, to love.

The Invisible World reveals to us this Truth within its silence.

How many hours, minutes, or seconds do you think you live in the Invisible World? Meditate on this. Realize that you are creating your entire Life from this dimension and manifesting it in the physical world -- a world comprised of the densest realms of vibrating matter. In the material world, this energy is condensed and trapped. It is all an illusion.

Once we identify and dwell in the "sacred space of the Most High," from which our feelings, thoughts, and emotions arise, we can then learn to understand and control them. As a result of identifying how and from where we are creating our daily lives, we start living with Awareness. Awakening to the Light, we plainly see that all we co-create is our responsibility.

Every second vibrates within our Present moment, our now. In one split second of awareness, we can create a Life full of Light, Joy, and Love.

Live now, enjoy Life now! Love now, for this now is the precious moment that is creating our lives. Each now is unique -- it won't come back in time. In it we leave a footprint, and within that impression are the actions we leave behind. Each step we take, we leave a mark. The path is created by the steps a person takes while walking it.

The Present Moment connects us to the Zero Point. All within Creation exists here and now. It is all right in front of you. It is a Gift if you decide to receive it, to live and experience all, to create and achieve all you desire, and to give and receive Love.

I invite you to reflect: look for your Balance in Life. Recognize the living force within you, cherish and guard your Inner Peace and Happiness.

Never give your Peace away to any person or situation. Nothing is worth losing it!
Meditation will help you discover the gift that your Creator has given you. Your joy will be found in sharing it with others.

You can be a transmitter of Fear or an envoy of Peace and Love. Which do you choose to be?

To live in ever greater consciousness is to awaken to your life's purpose.

Your awakening and your vibration stimulate other individuals to rise. Your Light is like a candle in a dark room. When it is piercing the darkness, its light is small, but the darkness is no match for it. Energy flows. The force of Light manifests without resistance.

One candle can light thousands of candles and lose none of its luster.

When you discover this truth, you will understand that you possess the potential to be that candle, that you can and will *enlighten* yourself and others.

My Notes:

_____

_____

_____

_____

The Architect of Your Own Destiny © 1983 Jacqueline Ripstein

Lesson II

The Architect of Your Own Destiny©

"When we are no longer able to change a situation, we are challenged to change ourselves." Viktor E. Frankel.

Our Life is our best work of Art.

We are creating it every moment.

God gives us Life.

Our journey begins at birth.

Every day, every second is a new opportunity
to create the Life we desire.

Death is not the end.

How we create our lives depends on us. By taking responsibility for
our actions, we take the reins of our own lives into our hands.

We are our best friend, but we can also be our worst enemy.

Tests come to us to help us dissolve our egos and their vast shadows
that veil our Light.

Step by step, we recreate ourselves.

Our life takes on new meaning when we infuse it with
Forgiveness and Love.

This lesson reveals the second step to awareness, as you learn to put your attention and intention into who you truly are and realize how you want to re-create your life. You will learn and discover that you are none other than the manifestation of your own thoughts, the product of your decisions, and the consequence of your actions. You possess free will; you are free to choose and design your own path. Create your Life as you would like to live it now, in this Present moment. Do not let Life pass you by. We all have a purpose, a calling. Each second that passes by cannot be recaptured.

Our past decisions, thoughts, words, and actions are what makes us who we are today. In our Present moment we are shaping our future.

Every action we take shapes our lives. In our every act, no matter how small, we are sculptors, chiseling bit by bit. Just as a diamond takes form out of a piece of dark coal, and the inner beauty of a precious stone is revealed when subjected to high temperatures and incredible pressure, so too is our inner light released from the dense iron grip of ego. That is, like the diamond that is cut and polished by outside forces so that it may shine, our lives are also shaped and polished by life lessons.

Intense pressure, followed by cutting and shaping, is what brings forth the diamond's energy, its angular facets reflecting and refracting Light. In the same manner, a human being is polished and the ego's darkness dissipates as we learn from the many challenges and lessons of life. Each test reveals our inner strength as life provides a continuous circuit of tests, one embedded within the next until we pass the final test ... and realize who we truly are, reflecting the Light of the Creator within us.

Who gives Life to the sculptor and who gives Life to the sculpture?

Learning to Love ourselves is not easy. We often identify more with our darkness than with our Light. When we nourish our lives with Joy, Love, and

Faith, our inner self becomes stronger. When we live in this way, life's tests become fewer, and our suffering diminishes.

We often hate, judge, and resent the people who are testing us, those who make us suffer. But in the same way that a diamond is polished by friction from another diamond, a person grows from interaction with another person. These people who test us are instruments of Life; they enable us to grow and learn about our own lives, helping us discover our darkness as they help us reveal our Light.

When a diamond remains uncut, it does not shine.

Every thought we hold in our mind and speak with our mouth manifests in our physical reality as we walk along the path of Life.

"The sculptor removes all that is superfluous and reduces the material to the form that exists within the artist's mind." Giorgio Vasari (1511- 1574).

When we are afraid, we attract situations that cause us to be even more fearful. Lack of love -- including fears, low self-esteem, depression, and ill will -- attracts some of the stones and potholes that we encounter along our path, and we continually trip and fall over and into them. But they too serve a purpose: they test us, and we either become paralyzed by them, having surrendered our inner strength to them and failed the test, or we overcome them in a triumphant way, passing the test and coming out even more strengthened to overcome the next one. Just like the diamond that is released from coal under great pressure, with each lesson learned, we gradually emerge. With each breath, we are given the opportunity to grow, to awaken to our true Being, to start reflecting our inner light.

As you are being tested, try to identify the dynamics of your test. Acknowledge the challenges, look within yourself, and with self-honesty notice the dark spots to be treated, those that need to be converted into Light. Face them head-on and they will start disappearing from your life.

Our thoughts and feelings have vibrations of energy that connect to the corresponding vibrations of the universe. This energy sends back to us exactly what we think and feel — the positive and the negative. All that we are, now and in the future, we are creating in this *Present* moment.

When we accept responsibility for our own actions and act like "mature" human beings, this new awareness enables us to grow in the Presence of each test. If we don't get through it and somehow "blow" our opportunity, the same test will continually return to us. We will keep right on digging the same holes for ourselves to fall into and gravitate to the very same stones to trip over, until we learn the lesson. Only then can we move on to the next lesson.

So I ask you: *How much time do you want to spend on the same lesson?*

To master a Life test, first recognize that it's indeed a test and understand that the possibility of its recurrence lies within you.

To pass a test, you need to find within yourself the energy that is creating that test.

As soon as you can identify these tests as dark energetic obstructions that are active within and need to be cleared away, you can transcend them. You will then rise to higher levels of Consciousness. All failed tests simply return to us through other people and circumstances. These people and things may have different names, but the same dynamics will repeat themselves until you confront them by mastering any darkness within yourself, transmuting and conquering the mind, feelings, thoughts, and actions. Every self-conquering step brings you to higher states of Consciousness. Tests are of course not only of the interpersonal kind, but come in many other ways as well, such as sickness, loss, and accidents. All of Life is a continuous trail of self-imposed tests.

The mastery of our lives lies in how we face and transcend its tests.

Whether we learned and passed or freaked out and flunked, the question remains: To what degree did we face the test or hide from it? Did we pass to a higher level of awareness and Consciousness, or did we stagnate? Might we have even devolved? If we've failed, then the same test will come back to us as many times as we need to learn it; if we've passed, new tests will appear. Until we pass a test, any new or more advanced ones will not appear. The tests of Life are steps along the way to our Divine Being.

Question: *So then, how do we see through the shadows within ourselves to find that unresolved negative energy that keeps attracting a complementary test?*

Answer: *Simply by detecting what it is that we don't like to face, by becoming aware of situations that keep coming back to us. If we are stubborn and blind, Life comes knocking at our door with its repetitive, negative tests until we accept they are there to free us.*

As we enter our *Invisible World* through a process of focusing our thoughts and feelings within the True Self, we can easily locate our dark, egoic energies. These are the negative feelings that turn into thoughts that bring us constant suffering. Feeding off the dark shadow energy, it is these thoughts that if not confronted will keep attracting undesired situations into our lives. Once we take a good, honest look at the emotions inside us, and become aware of all shadow energies that nourish the darkness, we can then begin to open up to transformation. Only then can we grow emotionally and spiritually; only then can we reach a state of higher Consciousness. From the time of our birth, Life has programmed lessons to teach us, based on the

DNA of our Souls. We were all created with a purpose. Every individual Life has a specific *invisible blueprint* that dictates the different experiences and tests that will occur. All that happens is for our learning and growth.

The Creator gives us Life. We are born with particular tastes, with a personality that defines us as human beings. Still we must understand life's lessons in order to realize the perfection of our Being, to bask in the reflection of our Light.

From this lesson we learn that: We are the *"Architects of our own Life,"* that we are co-creators. God gave us free will, and we are therefore responsible for our every action, our every word, and our every thought. Sometimes it's hard for us to believe this -- our ego passionately denies it! Our task is to unmask the ego and penetrate its shadows. In order to do this, we must redirect the very same energy that the ego drains from us so that we may create our lives as a masterpiece of Light.

Michelangelo, the great artist of the Renaissance, said: *"Like a chisel on marble, I remove all that is not needed from the rock, so that little by little the figure that has been hiding inside the great piece of marble comes to Light and Life."*

In the sphere of human expression that we call artistic Creation, three qualities that are unique in this process are the representation, the transmission, and the transmutation of human feelings. Therefore, one of the essential roles of the Arts is to alleviate and release repressed and painful feelings from the most hidden depths of a human being.

Creative forces and our imagination are among the tools that we have to recreate our lives. One has to be brave and lose the fear of the unknown in order to reveal the sculpture that is locked within oneself.

As co-creators of our lives, our goal is to create a work of art made in the image and likeness of our Creator. This process will reveal our Truth. How we view ourselves must progressively shift away from the material world of appearances and flow toward the Truth, the Spirit world. It is not an easy task to redirect our focus away from the physical world and place it where eyes cannot see; it is the deep Invisible World that embraces our Spirit, our true identity. When we base our value on the "e-valu-ations" of the material world, we believe we are merely the block of stone and are blind to the sculpted Being of Light that blazes within that stone. We devalue our lives every time we think of ourselves as no more than a physical body, rather than an awe-inspiring Light Being created in the image of our Creator. This Soul, or energy Life within, is what gives us our magnificent Spiritual essence.

Our ego, which is always an illusion, gives us a false identity that obscures our true reality -- our Spirit, the Light and Energy that live inside our physical body. If we base our value as a human being on material belongings and physical endowments only, imagine how terribly undervalued we will be!

The sculpture looks so real that the observer will barely recognize the difference between the stone and the Life within the stone.

Reflections

With every step we take, we are clearing and creating our path.

The second step to our awareness is to place our full attention on who we truly are, thereby unmasking our egos and discovering our inner Light.

Upon deciding to be a sculptor, the artist makes preparations, choosing the materials and location to create his grand masterpiece. When we are born, we come into the world with a predestined program. As we grow we start creating and manifesting the circumstances of our lives through our actions. We choose our beliefs and then add our particular karma to the program we came in with. We may choose to upgrade or downgrade the program.

Love and compassion are innate to humans, they enhance our Divine Being.

Every action taken and every piece chiseled is the sole responsibility of the sculptor alone, and no one else. Take full responsibility for your creations! Take inspired risks! Use your intuition, and know that there is a force of unimaginable greatness inspiring and guiding you at all times.

Eliminate all sculpted creations that are unlovely and useless. Don't save them as sad mementos or pieces for future repair. Don't be burdened by them. Throw them away.

As we create our masterpiece – our Life – we need to chisel and, little by little with each strike, discover parts deep within ourselves that we have never seen before.

We are all learning in the *School of Life*. The lessons are lovingly designed in the master plan for our education and our growth while we are in this material plane.

We are both the sculptor and at the same time, the great work being created.

God creates our lives, we co-create them.

In the Whole, there is no separation. Even the energy that the sculptor uses is transferred to his work and remains vibrating inside of it.

The vibration of Love in a masterpiece will be felt by anyone who has the sensitivity to perceive it.

The co-creator has the capacity to know that inside of him are the qualities and inner strength necessary to be triumphant.

Discover who you are. Reconnect with your Light and recognize your Inner Strength. Identify and experience your emotions. Discern and refine your thoughts, and be in the place of power as you become the Architect of your own destiny.

Your actions and decisions play the leading role in constructing the masterpiece that is your life.

Love and Compassion are your tools to chisel your Life.

I invite you to discover the sculpted Light figure hidden within you.

My Notes:

_____

_____

_____

_____

Life © 1987 Jacqueline Ripstein

Lesson III

Life©

Everything flows out and in. Everything has its tides. All things rise and fall.
The pendulum swing manifests in everything. The measure of the swing to
the right is the measure of the swing to the left. Rhythm compensates.
The Kybalion

The boat symbolizes our journey through Life, our journey through
the physical world.
The ocean symbolizes Spirituality and Life.
A calm ocean represents a state of inner Peace and emotional balance.
A turbulent ocean symbolizes pain, anxiety, stress.
Life is a Spiritual journey.

51

$\mathcal{L}$ife's high tides and storms make us feel beaten. We may face death, loss of health, loss of wealth, feel pain or anger, or both. When we experience any of these tests, we often feel *despair*.

In this lesson we encounter our third level of awareness...Life itself! As we encounter Life's many tests, we get closer to discovering our Spirit, our true self that lives in our Invisible World. When we awaken to know our Spirit, then the trials, storms, and tests of Life will not crush us.

Our Spirit is Eternal and nothing can destroy it.

The tide represents the back and forth swing of emotions that we are constantly experiencing in our lives. Sometimes we find ourselves up, and sometimes we are down. The times that we are down represent an opportunity to move up again.

The ocean is Life and movement. The salt water of the sea is contained in our tears; it is the water of the maternal womb.

Take a moment to reflect. Breathe . . . reflect on the painting of Life. What do you see?

The sky reflects the forces of Light, Faith, Joy, and Hope. This Light is ignited within us. As we recognize it, we glean the knowledge that Life is worth living.

The wind blows slowly, caressing the water that moves with the flow of Life. The sun nourishes and gives Life to everything, including the ocean. The water comes and goes; the vast sea of Life rocks us with its flow. Emotions swirl, seconds pass, spring and winter, Life and Death. All endings represent a new beginning.

There is calmness, but suddenly chaos enters our lives, and we are not always prepared. The wind blows stronger and the waves begin to roar with force and rise with the invisible energy that drives them. A storm has been created. Its force destroys everything in its path. Life at that moment is testing us. Powerful, unconscious feelings arise and uncertainty or painful situations begin. The trials have started.

In this lesson we are receiving the "anchors" to avoid the drifting of "our boat" and our lives.

A storm is often necessary to unmask the ego, to destroy the masks that we have unconsciously created by our need to protect ourselves. We try to pretend that we are perfect as we cover up our fears of being judged or talked about by others. Our low self-esteem covers itself with a million masks. We disguise the greed, egoism, anger, rage, pain or hate that we may feel. A storm is needed to help cleanse all of this energy from our lives and unburden us. The destruction caused by the storm unmasks the world of illusions we have created and leads to the construction of a new Life.

Growth requires forgiveness as we reconstruct our lives. First, we must forgive ourselves, knowing that we are doing the best we know how, accepting that we are the creators of our lives. Our "mistakes" are but guidelines leading us onto the right track. As we confront ourselves with humility, we must understand that all experiences also help exalt our lives.

Beauty is in the eyes of the beholder. We see Life in the Present moment through the different experiences we have had in our lives. It is important to recognize that we are doing the best that we can within the realm of what we know. We can only overcome a problem from the level of Consciousness we have at the Present moment. But Consciousness continues to grow. One step takes us to the next, and one level of Consciousness will trigger the next one in a never-ending process. As we grow, we awaken to new realities of our own Being. We become more responsible for our own actions, and this sense of responsibility enables us to respond in better ways when a storm hits. Darkness gives us the opportunity to understand that what we are really aiming for is Light, a Life of Peace, Empathy, Compassion, and Love.

Drifting from the Present moment can cause us to lose focus in the real world; the world of illusion traps us again and again.

Our lives can be symbolized by a boat. Often we are afraid of the vast ocean of Life, afraid of facing the storm and its destruction. How many times have we felt that there was nothing more we could do, that we were drowning in weariness and pain? When we lose hope and faith we have lost our survival tools.

After we experience pain, tragedy, loss, and setbacks, we become more alive and often without realizing it, we take a step upwards toward the Light. In the painting of Life in this lesson, we see the ***Boat of Life*** destroyed. Its fragments float and the pieces drift apart, reminding us of the fragility of Life. We feel destroyed, empty, drifting in pieces. We doubt we can move forward. When we view the painting under the Invisible Light, then we see that the boat is still there, complete. We awaken to the Truth within us. ***We know we are safe, our Spirit is complete…we Survive.*** No *test* can really destroy us. The Soul, our Spirit, is Eternal.

Exhaustion limits us and affects our health, crippling our ability to continue the struggle to overcome adversity. Worries drown us, turning us into victims as we steer ourselves to negative experiences through our own fears and thoughts. We believe these thoughts are the Truth.

Life © 1987 Jacqueline Ripstein

Same painting seen under Black Light.
Invisible Art and Light Technique © Pat

Life © 1987 Jacqueline Ripstein

Same painting seen under Normal & Black Lights.
Invisible Art and Light Technique © Pat

When will we recognize that we are our own worst enemy? Impotence, fed by indifference and weakness, causes us to lose our inner strength and become swept away by the noise and negativity that feed us daily. Winning the battle comes from the conquest within. When we achieve inner Peace, it becomes possible to separate ourselves from aggressive situations, war, and anguish.

Are we living or merely existing? *Faith* enables us to *conquer* Life's challenges. Faith is our survival mode. Without Faith, Life becomes meaningless and we find ourselves relating only to the material world. To be alive means to take risks so we can navigate through the sea of Life. It is to journey with fluidity, adapting to changes as they present themselves. It is to accept Life's tests instead of resisting or opposing them, thanking them for giving us an opportunity for growth. It is to decide to swim and not drown, to not resist as we learn to flow. **As we flow, we will discover Peace and serenity within us, and our hearts will open to Life itself.**

When we lose our connection to our Spirit, we lose the breath of Life.

The heart beats, resonating with the pulse of Life. Everything rises and falls as part of the beat of Life. In the physical world nothing remains static; everything has vibration and movement. The ups and downs of emotional waves lift one's being in times of Peace and joy, and lower it in moments of pain and suffering. In Life's constant movement, there are declines or times of unsteadiness to show us that these experiences are also necessary to celebrate a reason to awaken to Life. The times of pain and challenges are temporary, and they will disappear when we are able to transform them. Everything will pass.

Dawn comes after a dark night, and the sun shines once again to illuminate a beautiful day before us. Each day represents a blank canvas, and each of us is responsible for creating our own masterpiece every moment of our lives.

Mother Earth is our teacher. I invite you, in the silence of your Being, to perceive Life's messages of beauty and existence. Take a moment and watch the clouds, listen to the wind, listen to the birds – be alive. Pay attention, since the messages are often hidden in places where you least expect them.

Animals are here to help us, to guide us.
They are part of our Life's journey.

I will never forget an experience I had several years ago. I was about to sign a contract but was very afraid to do so. My intuition clearly told me not to sign because the people with whom I would be working were wolves dressed in sheep's clothing. Insecurity overwhelmed me, my low self-esteem drowned me, and my fears controlled me.

The morning before I was supposed to sign the contract, a raven landed on my balcony. Its small black eyes sought my eyes as if it wanted to talk to me. A message from Mother Nature was being delivered to me, but I was too busy, too focused, too embedded in my fears to stop and listen. I could clearly see that the bird's small right foot was broken. For a few seconds, the bird stared intensely at me; then it turned and flew off.

That same day while I was recording a television program, I fell and broke my right foot – the same side as the poor crow's. With a rod in my foot, and supported by my fears, I signed the contract the next day and got myself involved with the wrong people.

Mother Earth – through the bird – was trying to keep this painful experience from happening. My dread about signing the contract manifested itself when I broke my foot. The broken foot demonstrated how afraid I was of "stepping into the future." That experience showed me that a storm was drawing near. I could have avoided it if I had been more aware of my fears and had listened to Life's messages. My low self-esteem and my fears attracted the low-energy situation of breaking my foot.

If my consciousness had been awake and alert, if I had understood that nothing positive could come from a state of insecurity and fear, such a painful experience would never have happened. Neither would the raven with the broken foot have appeared.

It is important that we be alert to recognize the signals that announce danger is imminent. A storm does not come from nowhere. It forms slowly before an atmospheric change or at the convergence of different temperatures. The black clouds come closer, little by little. Another signal is the intensity of the changes of color in the sky. These colors also exist within our emotional states of mind.

In Life many storms form clearly before our eyes. Because of our busy schedules, the constant noise and fears, we ignore the birds that take flight to seek shelter. As in the case of the devastating tsunami in Indonesia in 2004, according to eyewitness accounts, many people ignored the screams of the elephants that turned around and ran for higher ground, heading away from the waters before the wave hit the shore. How many people would have survived if they had followed their intuition as the animals did?

The wind begins to blow and pick up speed. The storm intensifies and the waves swell. The wind fuels the waves and drives them with force. A storm energy is triggered. Our lives are shaken before attacks of the tempest. Is it possible to recover from the storm? How much longer will we be able to resist? There is nothing that human nature cannot overcome. These tests are a way of measuring our inner strength. However challenging the test may be, we possess the necessary inner strength to overcome it. No more, no less.

The storm brings about different kinds of losses. Deterioration of one's health, continuous pain, the loss of a loved one or of material possessions, all of these touch our lives and affect our behavior. When we convert what we see as negative and focus it into a positive, we can understand that all sicknesses have something to teach us. It is when we turn our focus within, understanding and growing with each storm, that we pass the test. If in our minds we feel destroyed before the storm even hits us, then we are already defeated.

In the moment the storm appears, if we have not identified and overcome inner weaknesses and if fear invades our being before we confront the adversity, then defeat is inevitable. The storm will lash out without pity. As the boat yields and becomes shipwrecked from the force of nature, the feeling of hopelessness impedes one's ability to progress and overcome the calamity. The pain is too strong and the heart grows weak. Suddenly, we believe that Life has been extinguished. We cannot go any further.

Behind the darkness, however, there is always Light. In spite of their destructive power, storms also contribute something positive...Blow by blow, they annihilate the world of illusion, and one by one, they break the egos that falsely fortify our being. Step by step, we uncover the magnificence of our Essential Self.

But what does it mean to be destroyed? What part of our Being feels destroyed?

Just as the ego breaks and melts away in the presence of the Light, the Spirit is unbreakable and nothing can destroy it. When the ego and its vast forces stagger and lose strength, the rays of Light begin to shine. Energy rises up and feeds inner strength, allowing the Being to vibrate at the highest frequencies of Light. The destruction of our lives as portrayed by the shattered boat exposes the many fears and shadows that veil our Light.

When a loved one dies, it is important to know that their vibration has passed from this Life to a higher one. The being can never cease to exist even though the body vanishes. The vibration of the Soul continues its journey. If in our lifetime we create a higher energetic charge through our actions, then we continue our journey to a place of higher vibrations – a place of Peace and Love. In this place, there is no room for low vibrations; there is no rancor or bitterness.

Conversely, if the actions in a lifetime convey low energy experiences, then when we leave our bodies that energy vibration defines us, attracting us to the dimensions that match that vibration.

Do we experience Life's challenge with rancor or with faith and forgiveness?

I invite you to discover the secrets of the Invisible World, the world where your Spirit exists, from where you are creating your Life. Listen to your inner messages. When you feel depressed, return to the image that reveals the Invisible boat and observe.

In the Invisible World you will see that the boat appears intact. Like your Spirit, it can never be destroyed. The Soul is eternal.

Here is a brief meditation that can help you connect with your Higher Self. Take three slow breaths. Be aware of your breathing; listen to your breath. Concentrate on this *Present* moment, allowing the stillness of your Spirit – *the Invisible boat* – to inspire you. Listen to the whisper of the ocean waves. Calm the water of your body, relax and feel Peace within you. See the Light illuminating everything. The boat is composed of this Light.

The human body, like the wooden boat, is merely the vehicle to create the experience of Life. If at a given moment, we think about death as an alternative to Life, then we have not felt Life. The only death we can encounter is to be dead while we are alive, to walk through Life in an automatic way as if we are asleep. In this state, we lose Life's beauty; we are connected only to the material world, unaware of the existence of our Spirit.

> *Death and Life are two polarities,*
> *both vibrating within Life's experience.*

Death is not the end of a Life; it is the culmination of a lifetime. At the moment of birth we inhale and at the instant of death we exhale. This is the Cosmic rhythm – inhale, exhale. Breathing keeps us alive and connected to all living things. The first action of a newborn is to breathe in: *in spiritus,* the Spirit enters Life. When we have moments of inspiration, the first thing that happens is that we unconsciously take a big breath in; in that second we connect with our Spirit. Breathing is a way to merge our body, mind, and Spirit. When we are stressed, our breathing gets shorter, and sometimes we forget to breathe. When we release stress, we exhale.

The Creator provides the strength and wisdom to face Life's circumstances. But it is essential to hoist the sails continually to navigate Life's tests as they occur, and to accept that the inner Being is prepared for everything and has what it needs to face Life's most difficult challenges.

Struggles are instruments that help us grow. They are opportunities, not obstacles – they are times to improve ourselves and learn. We have the power to choose how we will react to Life's challenges. Believe in yourself. Value your Being and give it the respect it deserves.

There are no challenges that are impossible to address. The tests present themselves because we possess the capability to resolve them. Everything in Life that we attract to us contains the same energy that lies inside of us; otherwise it would not present itself. Each test has a specific purpose, and therefore it happens to us and not to others. We must discover that purpose; observe what we are learning with the tests that confront us. If we search deep within ourselves, we will find a weak spot, a place where we might feel undeserving, unloved, defeated, in pain, angry with ourselves. The ego rejoices in these low vibration feelings and is nurtured by them. To cleanse ourselves from this energy, we attract people and situations that emphasize the feelings we contain deep within us – feelings we have when we love, value, and nurture ourselves, when we free ourselves from outside criticism. As we start losing our fears, our inner strength ignites, and our lives start changing.

Look beyond the five senses and activate the invisible sixth sense within you. Your intuition is an essential tool for survival. It is our guide in moments of Darkness and is ignited by our Spirit.

Pain is not a choice; suffering is a choice. The feeling of destruction is created when we see the glass as empty rather than full of Light. Even when the clouds cover the Light, the Light is always shining. Beneath suffering we find impotence and fear impeding our ability to recover.

When we regain Love and faith we start a new Spiritual journey. We connect to our inner strength to pass all tests and reach our goals. At the end of this Life, we don't take anything with us pertaining to the material world. Rather, we carry a bag full of actions and experiences that enrich us beyond any material fortune.

Our goal is to be able to overcome any test. It is to enjoy Life, elevate ourselves to grandeur, **awaken** our Consciousness, and overcome illusion without losing any faith. It is to ask ourselves before each storm: *"Is it true that this storm can destroy me?"*

Listen to the answer in the silence of your heart.

Reflections

The third lesson is teaching us about life itself.

When we focus beyond the five senses, we are able to activate our Invisible sixth sense, our Intuition. This is our guide in moments of darkness and danger. Awaken it, listen to it, use it.

Challenges present opportunities to make corrections and see Life in a different way. They create the opportunity for us to grow and change and allow us to appreciate and reveal what we know and have. As we awaken to our Spirit's existence, *the Light in our eyes shines with the Divine spark that is part of the Creator's Light.*

Pain is not a choice; suffering is a choice. The ego attaches us to pain while blinding us to Joy.

We have a tendency to see the glass of water as half empty and miss that the "empty" is full of Light. The feeling of being destroyed causes us to lose faith; we focus on our darkness and not our Light. Even when the clouds cover the sun's Light, the sun always shines. Although we don't see our own Light, it always shines inside us; we must remove the layers of darkness and unmask the Light.

Behind pain we find impotence and fear. This situation brings us more pain. Impotence makes us believe we don't have the ability to raise ourselves up to accept our own strength. We feel safe within our comfort zone and we freeze with fear at the thought of leaving it. Many times it's more comfortable to stay sleepy and sheltered in suffering and fear than to break away from these low-vibration energies. *As we change our focus from our pain to our strength, a spark of Light that is part of the Divine Light activates within us, giving us more strength than we could ever imagine.*

*S*torms and challenges are instruments that appear in order to help us grow. They are opportunities, not obstacles. They are moments in which to improve and learn. Our goal is to overcome any test, to enjoy Life, to rise up to the grandeur of who we are as our Consciousness awakens.

It is to ask ourselves before every storm: "Is it true that this storm and test can destroy me?" Listen to the answer in the silence of your heart.

Wake up every day and be grateful to be alive. Let your Spirit travel through the course of your Life, because living through the awareness of the Spirit will bring only reward to your Life.

Don't leave Life without saying goodbye, without saying I Love you, without saying thank you, without offering a hand to someone who has fallen. Don't walk through Life without sharing Life's riches, without sharing your Light and Love.

Smile and you will see that many smile with you. Remember that it is always darkest just before dawn.

The Light always shines!

My Notes:

_____
_____
_____
_____

The Burden of Life © 1980 Jacqueline Ripstein

Lesson IV

The Burden of Life©

"Hope is like the sun which as we journey toward it, casts the shadow of our burden behind us." Samuel Smiles

The purpose of Life is not to have achieved success by the end of our lives, but to succeed as we live.

Every Human Being is unique.

Our thoughts incite actions, our actions manifest our reality. We alone are responsible for our own actions; there is nobody to blame.

Every person carves out his or her own destiny.

The more burdens we carry, the more arduous the ascent, and the slower we advance.

Every decision we make carries a consequence. One must simply evaluate the price to be paid in that consequence.

Learning from every test of Life leads us to the mastery of our lives.

Those who have succeeded have thoroughly recognized the immense importance of the Divine plan.

$\mathcal{E}$verything happens for a reason. Nothing happens by chance. There are no coincidences, only causes. Every action creates a reaction. With our actions we initiate a chain of events that occur in perfect order according to the *Law of Cause and Effect*. Without exception, we experience all the consequences of all our actions.

The fourth lesson guides us to learn about Life's purpose and to help us revise the burden we tend to carry. It will teach us to question ourselves about our life's objective and to focus on creating an intention in all that we do. Life offers many kinds of experiences: joyful, loving, fun, and painful, the ups and downs. They all are part of our life journey. Step by step we create our lives.

The path is created simply by walking it. With every negative action such as stress, worry, anger, and anxiety, we accumulate a heavier load to carry. Some people talk about being on a spiritual path, yet they have wandered away from that path. In order to walk the path, our thoughts, words, and deeds must be congruous, they must match up. *"If you're going to talk the talk, you've got to walk the walk."*

A life well lived has nothing to do with reaching the top of a mountain, but rather is present in every step we take as we, with others, enjoy what we are creating. The Mastery of Life lies in our walk, the step-by-step progression, the rising after every fall. We learn not by falling, but by how we stand up after a fall. It is not an easy task to conquer our fears, the ego, runaway emotions, and negative thoughts. Every test we learn from is a victory over our own worst enemy - our ego-selves. How do we take each step? Are we happy, with a "spring" in our step? Or do we "drag our heels," depressed, angry, or sad? Do we take responsibility for impressing our own footprints? Are we leaving traces of love in other people's hearts? Or are we still trapped in the past? If so, then the present moment is passing us by. Are we present and passionate about our Life? Only we can walk our path to success.

The road to God is always under construction.

The pitfalls, pratfalls, and reversals are there to help us become stronger and more aware. With every step upward in consciousness, we get closer to the Divine within.

"O God! My load is so heavy. How it weighs me down! I'm not sure I can endure it..."

I called this painting ***"The Burden of Life."*** *It demonstrates how each of us carries our own sack of experiences. It is up to us to make the load heavy or light. Be aware, and keep only those experiences in your sack that nurture you and bring you joy. Relinquish those experiences that only create more burdens. Understand what these experiences have taught you and let them go; they belong to the past.*

Each sack is like no other — it is full of valuable human experiences uniquely designed by each of us. These experiences are meant to help us master our Life's journey and to make it brilliant and exciting. ***Exciting?*** Yes, because Life's trials help us perceive our Light. Through awareness, we realize enlightenment.

There is a universal principle of cause and effect, action and reaction, a Law of Energy that governs all life. The consequence of our actions is called Karma or Dharma, the sum total of our good or bad actions, and sooner or later we will have to answer for these consequences. Our present actions are creating our future.

We ourselves are responsible for our own happiness and misery. If one sows evil, one will reap evil; if one sows goodness, one will reap only goodness. We create our own Heaven. We create our own Hell. We often ask ourselves why really bad things happen to really good people. My belief is that even if we are good we still have to polish ourselves; we are born with certain "karmas" that we need to clean.

I invite you to examine your sack, sorting through your "things" and assessing the load you are carrying. Check to see what is worth carrying and what is not. You may ask yourself: "Is this particular 'memento' still needed in order for me to be happy?"

Life's experiences of Joy, Love, Service, Empathy, and Compassion are positive feelings. They are not burdens, they do not weigh us down. They represent the energy we need to charge our enthusiasm and "lighten up."

If the load does not serve you, let it go. Discard all negative experiences and carry with you only Life's positive experiences. Bitterness, pain, resentment, and anger are heavy. They drag you down and resolve nothing. They chain you to the past. They belong to the shallows and shadows of our egos, not to our Light being. They limit our ability to walk – to grow – and our ability to ascend to higher levels of Consciousness.

Have you ever wondered what it would be like to change your burden for someone else's, or thought that another's Life would be easier and less painful than your own? It is very common for us to grow weary of Life's tribulations and wonder if our Life would be better if we turned in our sack for another. In other words, sometimes we may feel that the grass is greener in the neighbor's yard.

I ask you: Would you be willing to trade your load for someone else's, even knowing that it was specifically designed to help *you* master your own Life?

Would you be willing to lose your opportunity to grow in this lifetime?

Many times I have thought it might be better to trade my sack for a lighter one, but I always end up deciding that I prefer my own sack, even with its holes and patches, even though it may be heavy and uncomfortable to carry. Life is not as perfect as I envisioned it would be when I was younger, but I have learned that in imperfection lies the opportunity for growth. My sack contains the experiences I intuitively attracted in order to master my Life! I've cleaned it out many times. I have learned to let go of big dollops of pain and the heavy chunks of anger and resentment that anchored me to my past. At the end of our Life's journey, the experiences in our sack are the only possessions we take with us.

How many times do we try to carry the weight of others to help ease their pain? It hurts us to see their suffering, but our Love for them blinds us, and we can't see that through Life's journey we can carry only our own sack. Our loved ones' sacks are perfectly filled to help them master their own Lives. No matter how well motivated we are, by taking on even part of their own loads we debilitate them instead of helping them grow stronger.

It's easy to confuse one's sack with an anchor. Anchors represent moments of stagnation, when feelings and thoughts of inadequacy impede us from moving forward. When we are anchored in the past, the present moment eludes us. The rhythm of time continues, second by second, as the anchor lodges ever deeper into the mud, keeping us from moving forward. Although it may seem otherwise, the anchor has no power over us. *It is we who choose not to release it.* The power is within our own beings.

All beings create within their Invisible World the feelings and thoughts which later manifest in their Visible World. We alone are responsible for our experiences and their consequences. We alone bring them into our lives. It has been scientifically demonstrated that our thoughts affect our physical bodies. When thoughts come to mind and we uncritically accept them, it's usually too late to retract them. The thoughts have been inputted into our "computer program" and eventually will bring about an action. The action will be accompanied by a feeling. That is how we constantly manifest our *"reality."*

Our intuition, or sixth sense, is a direct perception of Truth, a gift that leads us not only to the good and the beautiful in life, but also to the discernment and avoidance of situations that can cause pain, even the kind brought about by Nature's catastrophic events. The constant noise that surrounds us, our stress, and our fears all block the channels of intuition and perception. We no longer use these channels and sometimes we even forget that we have them. Yet we can reclaim and foster our sixth sense if we focus on it, become aware of it, and listen to our intuition rather than our minds.

How to tell the difference between the voice of our mind and the voice of intuition? When intuition speaks, we may feel nervous, our heart beats faster – we have a *"feeling"* about something. We might even sense a *"don't do it"* thought. *By not following our intuition, we stumble into situations that could have been avoided.* If even only briefly we avoid Life's constant stress, we can then listen to the secrets of the Universe. An intuition is also called a hunch. Sometimes we can actually perceive an image, an intuitive perception of reality. Occasionally the stomach may even feel like it "crunches," as a feeling of uneasiness flows over our bodies. Listen to your body's language. These direct perceptions of reality are born in moments of sensitivity that connect us with our inner Being. The sixth sense reveals the hidden, Invisible World, while the rest of the senses connect us to the outer material world.

The intellect is connected to the ego. The more we listen to it, the more it throws its mesh over us, keeping us trapped. The first voice that speaks to us in any situation is our intuition. It reveals its Truth to us, while right on its coattails comes the voice of the ego, doubting or disregarding the first voice and implanting seeds of distrust that urge us to ignore our Spirit.

My artwork has revealed to me that the Divine Light of the Creator, the Angels, the Teachers, and Masters, are always Present, constantly guiding us along the road of Life and the Eternal path. Waiting for us to awaken in order to meet us, our Guides are infinitely patient. Mother Nature, with her Invisible and silent language, continuously guides us.

Reflections

This fourth lesson teaches us about our life's intentions, anchoring our lives in the true Spiritual Reality, liberating ourselves from the burdens that drag us down, and letting go of our fears, thereby focusing, and reconnecting to our Light.

We alone are responsible for all of the experiences and tests which we attract into our lives and which are the result of our thoughts and actions. There is no one else to blame.

Karma is not punishment; it's the consequence of natural acts. Karma means "deed" or "act" and more broadly names the universal principle of *cause and effect, action and reaction, a Law of Energy that governs all life.*

I believe that we are born with a destiny as well. In it we accumulate positive and negative, good and bad actions, which sooner or later produce results of the same nature. Our present actions are creating our future.

We ourselves are responsible for our own happiness and misery. If one sows evil, one will reap evil; if one sows goodness, one will reap goodness. We create our own Heaven. We create our own Hell.

***"If you're going to talk the talk, you've got to walk the walk."* Be completely honest with yourself.**

Thousands of thoughts flow into us. Some are fragments of our past experiences; many more we "pick up" and accept as our own. Be very careful about what thoughts you accept!

Observe your thoughts dispassionately. Discard those that bring you down. Replace them with positive, empowering thoughts.

When someone hurts or offends us, we have several choices: to avenge, to forgive, or to ignore. Our response depends entirely on the level at which our consciousness is at the time.

The one that gets "offended" is our ego, not our Spirit.

Any time you're in distress, take a moment to break from it and breathe three times, inhaling and exhaling slowly. Listen to your breath. Feel the touch of the breeze and the warmth of the sun. Smell the flowers, and bid them, "Good day!" Listen to the rapturous songs of birds and lift your head to watch the birds in flight. Protect the loving dolphins and whales, and all animals. And never forget the one who love you unconditionally – your dog.

Feel the beauty of Life as it vibrates within your Being.

Animals play an essential role as they accompany you on your Life's journey. They help you to realize that Love vibrates in all living creatures. Take care of them. They deserve our Love and respect.

Drop the illusion that the past continues as a reality in the present moment. Without your attachment to it, this most troubling of all illusions will vanish.

Obstacles are not there to stop you but to impel you to raise yourself up from the place where they were created. As you move beyond a challenging situation, more solutions appear. Know that you already contain everything within yourself to transcend *any* obstacle.

It is vital to go with the flow of the Universe, where time never stops. The Earth follows its course around the sun. The moon reflects the sun's Light. The planets dance to the rhythm of the Cosmos, following an Invisible Light vibration that guides all of Creation. Life vibrates in a rhythmic dance.

Why do we often remain in the past, living Life as if the past could continue into the Present? Why give it energy, when it is merely a phantom, consuming your precious Life energy?

Free will was given to us for our use. As its name suggests, it frees us to create as we will. And as we choose to take action in our lives, it is our privilege and duty to take responsibility for all of it.

It is the space between letters that brings words to life, just as the space between points can give rise to a line. Likewise, the space between our breaths connects us to the Infinite pool of Spirit, our true home.

The Light and energy that we radiate become sounds and colors, their vibrations emanating a silent language that all beings can perceive. Our wakefulness is a leap of joy between our innermost being and Mother Nature, between the body and the Spirit, between ourselves and God.

You are a being of energy that flows and connects with everything. This energy is a dance in and outside of time that makes the Cosmos and Life vibrate.

Enlightenment is the result of moving through Life with freedom and awareness, letting go of all that binds you and carrying fewer burdens by the day.

To be a being of "Light" means to be lighter and to radiate the brilliant Light of God that's within you.

Never doubt your intuition – listen to it. Believe in yourself; feel your Inner Strength. The past doesn't exist anymore. You are fully in the Present. Just like the seconds, the past evaporates.

Rise up to meet every day with your head held high, prepared to create a Masterpiece. Know that you contain within you all the wisdom and enlightenment you need to face any test before you. It is your gift to be alive, to be part of Life in all its splendor.

Recognize and express your strength, which is your Divinity. Be the co-creator of a new inner world of Peace and Love.

My Notes:

_____

_____

_____

_____

I Am © 1995 Jacqueline Ripstein

Lesson V

I Am©

"To be or not to be -- that is the question." **Shakespeare**

I Am Free

I Am Peace

I Am Love

I Am Service

I Am Compassion

I Am Eternal Love

I Am Light

I Am One with you

We strive to find who we are. We search all of our lives for our *Inner Being.*

*W*e travel to the most remote places on Earth searching for the correct answers. And what do we find? Nothing! Why do we find nothing? *Because our true Being is not who we are in the physical, material world. Our true Being is the Divine energy that manifests in our lives. It is hidden within us.* Within each one of us is where we can find all the answers to Life.

Attempting to be, we move farther away from being until we lose touch with our Inner Being.

This lesson guides us to a reunion with our Total Presence, to our true knowledge of who we are, and to our connection with our Inner Being. It is the connection with the Cosmic Consciousness of the "I Am." This lesson's intention is to remind us of, and to restore within us, the awareness of our Original Divine Nature. As we realize this Presence within us, we awaken to it.

The Mastery of Life is to realize that within us is Divine Being. Being exists in a state of Peace and Love.

Before the existence of man or animal, the Light vibrated, eager to create. There were no birds, fish, crabs, rocks, mountains, animals, plants, or forests. **There was only the Eternal Light, vibrating in every atom of existence.**

The sea was calm. The sky and heavens merged. Peace prevailed. Stillness reigned. The tranquil water and the winds joined in the Dance of Creation. The winds blew softly.

Eternal Life vibrates in and as everything. All of existence vibrates in this present moment.

The Earth and the heavens merged into an immortal "spark."

Humans were created with a sparkle and vibration of the Divine Light.

A seed of Divine Light was imbedded within us. It was the birth of the sacred self, the I Am Presence.

The I Am is the sparkle of God within us. We must awaken to this inner seed of Light. As we do so, it spreads its Light and its radiance, awakening others to the Light. Within this Divine Spark, the secret to the sacred identity of humanity remains imbedded in our mission. This mission is to express the Truth of Creation.

To Be...or not to Be...Is that really our choice?

The day of your birth arrived. You were born. *Like every human being, this unique new entity, you, arrived with great intrinsic worth and an individual identity.* There had never been anyone like you, nor would there ever be.

Being born is an act we experience as the *I Am* Presence enters a physical Life. A metamorphosis takes place. Our Spirit is born within a body to manifest its Divine spark in a material world.

Our goal in Life is to realize that we are Beings of Light, and in expressing that Light, our lives make a difference to this world. During childhood we still experience our essence as Light, but as we grow older, we forget. As we forget, we get confused and assume that we are mainly the body. In applying to our worth a material criterion, we devalue ourselves. The I Am Presence that shines within us patiently awaits our embrace.

At birth we come from The Light and at death we return to the Light.

Over the course of our lifetime, the noise, fears, and illusions constantly bedazzle and ensnare us. Gradually, we forget our essence and our true identity as the Divine Being that we are. Filling our lives with burdens, clutter, and noise, we begin to follow a certain programming of the mind.

I Am © 1995 Jacqueline Ripstein

Same painting seen under Black Light.
Invisible Art and Light Technique © Pat

This is a state of being in which we live on automatic pilot. We follow and become comfortably familiar with the "programs" that have been inculcated into our minds and bodies since birth. We lose our awareness of self-worth. This allows fears and doubts to invade our thoughts and emotions to the point where we become weak, easily manipulated, like not-so-gentle lambs needing to follow an authority figure. All of the low-vibrational programs of war, hatred, revenge, and jealousy feed our egos. Our Light energy is blunted and obscured by the ego's vast army of shadows and specters from the past. Reality is concealed, as confusion takes over. We believe we are the body because it seems so concrete and expressive, while overlooking the Spirit that animates that body and gives it all meaning. The ego's shadows constantly beguile us. *As a result, all the stress, commotion, and vain hopes and fears keep us frenetically sleepwalking through Life, instead of opening our eyes and finally seeing.*

The I Am Presence is Eternal. Its Light and power shine away all darkness.

The experiences of Life enable us to grow, to awaken. The Light of our Being can penetrate and expose those dark places that the ego has created. And as ego is dispelled -- seen for the nothingness that it is -- the Light expands and becomes stronger within us, more brilliant each time it exposes the lie in the shadows of the ego. As we pierce through these veils of illusion, we experience Enlightenment.

When the sun shines in all its splendor, giving us Light and warmth, there are times when it seems to be absent. Even though it always shines, the dark clouds cover its rays. The ambience becomes abysmal -- cold and gray. This can affect our mood, making us feel depressed and as if the colors of Life have faded. But even through the coldest of nights and the bleakest of hours, we can remember that the Light of our Spirit keeps shining within us. Discover this Light! Beneath those dark clouds of fear, hostility, and depression we will find it. When we raise ourselves up above the dark clouds we encounter our Light.

A new identity, a new Consciousness is thus born as we experience the bliss of union between the human and the Divine.

Rational thought (left brain) is necessary and very useful in practical Life. Yet, it can impede access to higher levels of Consciousness and the experiences that bring realization of endless, infinite Truth. Our right brain is the orchestrator of our more creative, spiritual connections.

External influences and appearances deceive us. They are created and distorted by the illusion of a "physical reality." The illusion of the mind system is directed and operated from the shadowy domain of the ego. This illusion utterly deceives us, as we assume that the physical, material world is responsible for manifesting our lives.

The more we suffer, the more we feed these shadows. The more we feed these shadows, the more they gather within us. One shadow nurtures and attracts all others. Much like cancer cells, the shadows proliferate, invading our thoughts and emotions. They multiply and give false weight to the illusions of our "physical reality."

How do we pretend to know other people, or believe that we know them, if we don't even know ourselves?

Self-knowledge is limited by the clouds of fears and delusions that hide our Light and limit our mind. These shadows obscure our greatness, sabotaging success with strange misgivings. The fear of encountering something new (and thus, seemingly, unpredictable and uncontrollable) in our lives, of moving out of our comfort zone, can freeze us. It feels more comfortable to remain in a place where we feel safe and in control. Of course, this cozy glen happens to be where our misery and unhappiness are created and perpetuated. Our vastness then seems limited, and this false limitation reduces the joy and the infinite possibility of our glory, our Truth, and magnificence.

As we open to this reality, our Higher Being goes beyond the limitations of our mind. It is the real power, available to each person. This Inner Being represents the wise, loving, compassionate, powerful, and radiant you.

Take a moment to draw in three long breaths. Then relax and experience a calming silence. Let that Peace permeate your being. By connecting to the I Am Presence, you are merging into the sacred space of awareness.

Self-observation helps us to refocus within, to balance ourselves and to be in the present moment.

As we awaken we move from a realm of confusion to one of certainty and Peace.

Are you ready to see the rays of your Light, to merge with your Higher Self, to move from fear into Love? Your *I Am Presence* invites you in this moment, as you are reading these words, to take a chance and embrace your Inner Child, to discover your true self. You will never again feel alone. Entering into the Invisible World and discovering what is there, you will be pleasantly surprised to encounter your true self. You will commune with all of creation, vibrating as One with all Existence. Follow this road and you will find the Truth. Have a dialogue with your Spirit — *The I Am Presence.* Your "Inner Child" expresses itself within your Invisible Reality. It misses you and eagerly awaits your return. Be aware of this

I Am © 1995 Jacqueline Ripstein

Same painting seen under Normal & Black Lights.
Invisible Art and Light Technique © Pat

precious being within you, connect to it, appreciate it, and let it play. This is the authentic self that you have lost behind the smokescreen of Life's many distractions. As we release our fears and desperate attachments to thoughts, things, and people, we understand that in reality, fears and low thoughts are incompatible with our inner Light of reality and don't belong to us. They are vagrants, drifting by and looking for a place to take up residence. While control over material reality is often very limited, we may realize complete control over our own thoughts and actions. It is in loving our essence — the *I Am Presence* — that we are able to truly love and nourish others.

In the School of Life events, situations, and the people you have attracted to be part of your personal experiences are synchronized perfectly in order to teach you the lessons that need to be learned. They show you exactly what is needed to be successful in your Life. Human experiences very often include challenges that slowly lift the veils of darkness, allowing the rays of the Higher Self to shine through.

Poverty and wealth are states of mind determined by our attachment to the material world. The less we know, love, and recognize ourselves — our true Being — the less abundance (however we define it) manifests in our lives. The more we can see our greatness, our glory, and the reality of our Inner Being, the more our mind expands and the greater abundance we attract.

Inevitably, we get tangled in an all-consuming illusion created by the ego system — the dream that we live only in a material world. Intoxicated by this fantasy, we tend to value people according to their talents, physical attractiveness, and the material goods they possess. Inherent human value is almost entirely overlooked. Our true glory cannot shine through such illusions, and in this limited space we lose all awareness of the *I AM Presence.*

The true being is free of limitations … It is pure abundance; it is pure Love.

Our mission in this lifetime lies in discovering our true essence. Only then can we manifest a physical, spiritual, and emotional Life of Abundance, Love, Peace, and Light.

Your Life is itself a Masterpiece of Creation — a masterwork in which you are playing the principal role. Let your Higher Self guide you and define the energy vibrations that drive your life. Your physical being is the actor that must take full responsibility for its different roles.

When we say *"I am something,"* it presents a particular "identity" that a person is attached to: I am an artist, I am a singer, I am a professional, I am a doctor, I am a father, I am a mother, I am a brother, I am a spouse, I am a child ... But the fact is, we are actually none of those identities. They are only roles or representations that we assume in our lives. Generally, one plays multiple roles: I am a daughter, mother, teacher, artist, aunt, tall, dark-skinned person … I am, I am, I am ... Alas! This is exactly what I am *not*. Our true Being is pure Light; it is *One* and One only. It is outside of time, *Eternal... It is simply, I Am.*

Be wary of those who claim to be your guide, guru, master, or a mouthpiece for Truth. Your only true guide is your own Being of Light, an emanation of God and the Light of Eternal Creation.

Never give away your inner power, for it belongs to you alone.

How do we give away our Inner Power? When we connect only to our physical, material reality. Searching in that realm for our strength, and power, we become fragile and our unconscious state creates suffering and weakness. Agonizing tests appear, as we become captives of our "form" identity, forgetting our "formless" nature. Our true strength comes when our physical being connects fully with our Spiritual reality. In short, within this conscious state of recognizing these "two" attributes of who we are lies the answer for living a whole life with supremacy for all our days.

The visible and invisible realities of the physical and spiritual world are the dimensions where we live our lives. One is finite, the other infinite.

What we can see with our physical eyes is not the reality of the Spirit. This *I Am* reality is beyond our physical sight. It is a space where light atoms vibrate information and transmit it to the Universe. In this Invisible World there is stillness and Peace. Life vibrates!

The dormant state of unconsciousness connects us only to the physical world, while the awakened consciousness reveals our Spirit.

Our lack of inner connection is what makes us fall prey to personalities that seem to nurture inner needs hitherto unsatisfied. It is easy to follow charismatic teachers, leaders, or anyone who offers us the "perfect solutions or promises," thereby surrendering our inner strength in acts of so-called humility and submission. But we will not be aware that this is happening until we have discovered our inner strength and the Light within us.

Going out in search of the unknown generates fear. It is our feelings of smallness and insignificance that limit our expansion. Our shadows block our Light. The more fear we allow in, the more we are entrapped in a cramped dark space, limiting our growth. Within these confines, we are unaware of a world full of Light. In despair, many place their hope in a savior. As we breathe our Glory, life brings us to a place where we will blossom. When you recognize this reality, you will lose all fears.

The words *I Am* reflect the truth of our Being. They are the expression of our reality. ***Say the words in reverse, from right to left, and you will find the Truth of Being: I AM ... AM I?*** This takes us to the perennial question that initiates an unveiling of our Truth. ***Who Am I?*** We encounter a clue when we question our identity. As we understand that our reality is multidimensional and factor in the fifty to seventy thousand thoughts that some scientists estimate flow into our mind each day in this dimension alone, it becomes clear how difficult it would be not to get caught in them!

As these questions resonate in your mind, pay attention to who is posing them. Is it your inner voice? Is it your ego? When we focus attention on our inner Peace ~ through the process of meditation ~ our thoughts shift, transforming the noise into stillness. The *Being* within will whisper to you, as it constantly does, and this time you will be able to listen. This silence connects to the seed of all Life, wherein abides your True Self. We then become aware, awakened to our Spirit.

This powerful sentence, *I Am*, is more than a simple understanding. It is God alive: alive in me, in you, and in all that surrounds us. *I Am* is the purest articulation of the Divine on Earth. It is the Divine will of God acting through the individual.

Reflections

In this fifth lesson we are creating the intention to discover our true Being. As we do so, a sense of Peace permeates our body.

The Light of Creation, the Immortal "Spark," vibrates within all things in creation.

Birth is the instant in which the gift of Awareness is bestowed; it offers the possibility of our awakening. The baby knows more about being a sparkle of the Light of God than about believing he is the body.

Though it may seem so, there is never a time when we are NOT connected to infinite Truth – it's a matter of becoming aware of that, of "realizing" it.

Wake up to your source of inner power!

Whenever you hear yourself saying, 'I am a teacher,' or an accountant, or any other identity, refocus and remember who you really are. Go into stillness to let the I Am be the only Presence and Power acting.

I *Am* is Life Eternal, and indestructible. It is the extension of the Divine within us. It is the manifestation of Life. I *Am* is pure Love. I Am is the intelligence that guides us, the energy that moves within every person, providing the experience of Life. The Awareness of Spirit elevates us from an earthly being to a Divine Being, united with all of creation.

All sentient "beings" of creation are unique and have their own intrinsic worth, energy patterns, and identity.

I *Am* reflects the UNITY with God and with all seeming "others."

It represents the responsibility we all have to manifest a world of Light and not of darkness.

"I Am that I Am" is perfect harmony.

By trying to be, we overlook the Being.
Calmly take three breaths. Inhale and exhale to the count of 7. Between the inhale and the exhale lies the space where you will find the portal to your Divine Being. The moment of inspiration — when we inhale — occurs in the instant of awareness when we begin to live Life through connection to our Spirit.

Create the intention of recognizing your 'I Am Presence.'

Within the silence of Spirit you can hear its words of wisdom. You realize that you are the teacher who answers the questions, the pilot who is guiding you, the inner voice you have been hearing, the Light you needed to enlighten your path, the Beloved you have been seeking.

I Am Wisdom. I Am Peace. I Am pure Love. I Am your Light. I Am One with humanity.

I Am your Spirit. I Am your Eternal Being. I Am Love.

You are never alone.
I AM always within you.

My Notes:

_____

_____

_____

_____

The Cosmic Chess Game of Life © 1992 Jacqueline Ripstein

Lesson VI

The Cosmic Chess Game of Life©

"Everything is dual. Everything has two poles.
Everything has its pair of opposites: like and unlike are the same.
The opposites are identical in nature but different in degree. Extremes
meet. All truths are but half-truths. All paradoxes may be reconciled."
The Kybalion

Opposites attract:

Light / Darkness
Truth / Falsehood
Reality / Illusion
Love / Hate
Joy / Sorrow
Giving / Receiving
Peace / War
Ascent / Descent

Are we Awake or are we asleep?

YOU decide: Do you choose the road of Light or the road of darkness?

This painting reveals to us an essential lesson that helps us grow and realize the mastery of our minds as we learn to transmute lower mental states into higher ones. It's a guide that takes us from unconsciousness states of lack of understanding to conscious living. A lesson that will guide you to turn Dark times into "En-Light-ened" ones. As we learn to drop our egos and vanquish our fears, we rise above all tests of life. We adopt kinder and more inclusive thought processes that lead to the "high road" we want to follow. Learn to control your mind, to unlock your inner power, and you will manifest the life of your dreams.

Transmutation is a law that states that the stronger an energy force is, the more prevalent force will always succeed. So in essence, our feelings and state of mind, whether positive or negative, will add to the overall energy of the outcome of our lives. Any negative process, whether it is in a thought, feeling, or emotion, can be transmuted with consciousness into positive energy.

We always have the power to choose; we can stay where we are, go backward, or use the opportunity Life is giving us to progress and expand our Light.

The Cosmic Chess Game of Life has its own rules and laws of energy. Once you understand them, the game changes and greater Consciousness is activated. As you play the game, you begin to understand its nature. The universal laws vibrate. They are activated throughout Life. There is no way to avoid them. Knowledge will open the gateway to 'the path of Truth.' The "Cosmic game" reveals to us the true nature of Life, its energy forces, and the Creation of Life itself – all belonging to an Invisible World. Mastery of the mind is essential. In Mental Transmutation, we learn how to activate higher mental vibrations, instead of falling into lower ones in which we have little or no power over our thoughts and feelings.

As you ask yourself these questions, you will be guided to the portals of greater Consciousness:

"Who am I? Where did I come from?"

"How do I play the game of my Life?"

"Am I happy with the Life I have created?"

"What is my Mission in Life?"

"How much time do I still have? Do I take care of my health?"

Rules of the Cosmic Game of Life

The mastery of our minds is the art of changing and transforming our own mental states and life's conditions, as well as being responsible for how we create our lives, and how we influence others around us.

The Law of Transmutation always concerns two things of the same kind, but to different degrees. To transmute means to alter, to create a change. The two ends of a board might appear to be the same, but there are many degrees of vibration between the two extremes of black and white, of Light and darkness.

By understanding *The Principle of Polarity,* the truth that all manifestations have "two sides," "two aspects," "two poles," a "pair of opposites," with manifold degrees between the two extremes, is revealed.

By raising our vibrations, our low and heavy fears can transmute into the highest degrees of fearlessness. Even the lowest vibrations of hate may be transformed into the sublime vibrations of Love by a change in polarity. Courage may be transmuted into fear, and vice versa.

The scale of color reveals to us its higher and lower vibrations, from the low infrared frequencies that are invisible to the eyes; to the visible spectrum

The Cosmic Chess Game of Life © 1992 Jacqueline Ripstein

Same painting seen under Black Light.
Invisible Art and Light Technique © Pat

of red to the violet, beyond the violet we have the again invisible ultraviolet spectrum. Emotions and thoughts vibrate colors. Many times we call these two poles Positive and Negative. But Light and darkness, good and evil are poles of the same Unity, with many degrees between them.

Love is the positive pole to hate's negative, as courage is to fear's.

To master our lives is the goal of this game. Our Life's journey is undertaken, obviously, by a physical body; and to the degree that we can "listen to our inner-being," it's then guided by our Spirit.

The rules of the Game of Life are based upon the energy principles that rule all of Creation. We are not mere observers in this game, not helpless pawns these game, not helpless pawns. We are co-creators, producers, and actors. We are born with some predestined events in our life of Kharma and Dharma. We then create our Life's experiences. We are responsible for all of our actions and every outcome. Every step we take is ours. There are definite rules as we play the Game of Life. *By following them, we can balance our lives and maintain higher levels of vibrations that flow with the universe.*

Everything in existence is energy. All Creation is based on energy and vibration.

Our physical being and our Spiritual being exist at different vibrational levels of frequencies.

RESPECT yourself so you can respect others.

*LOVE y*ourself so you can love.

Live with integrity, and honor your word, for every day you will encounter yourself in the mirror of Life.

THERE IS NO VALUE in blaming anybody. We are capable of changing our lives in every instant, informed by what we learn from each Life experience.

The Cosmic Chess Game of Life © 1992 Jacqueline Ripstein

Same painting seen under Normal & Black Lights.
Invisible Art and Light Technique © Pat

THERE IS NO VALUE *i*n complaining about our parents, brothers and sisters, friends, partners, or loved ones. Whatever they do and say to us, they are teaching us, and thereby offer an opportunity for us to grow beyond our own limitations. If we learn something that is not positive, we should work to change or eliminate it. (Using the Law of Mental Transmutation allows us to change the focal point to the opposite of what it was.)

THERE IS NO VALUE in harming others. Our anger, hatred, and unforgiving states only poison us. Internal aggression drowns and suffocates us. We create a Life of war, stress, and no Peace. We lose our opportunity to grow and master our lives in this lifetime. It is not worth it. If we work arduously and flow with harmony, we obtain inner Peace.

THERE IS NO VALUE in lying or evading the Truth. We are Spiritual Beings, navigating a journey within the boundaries of a material Life. We travel through life, looking for something outside of ourselves when that something, that everything, resides within us right along. What gives Life to our bodies is the energy of our Souls.

THERE IS NO VALUE in judgment. Judgment is one of the hardest 'hurting energies' there are, and one of the most inflexible negative vibrations that exist. In modern society, judging and gossiping have become entertainment. Judging others without mercy or compassion masks our fear that others will discover our own flaws. We project the dark energy within us onto others. Eventually, by judging others, we harm only ourselves; that sharp energy boomerangs back to us with even stronger force than the one we used when we threw it.

What we judge in others, we harbor within ourselves ... If not, we could not see it.

THERE IS *NO* BAD or GOOD in Life. As Shakespeare's Hamlet observed, "There is nothing either good or bad, but thinking makes it so."

Our Life experiences are only experiences. We attract the ones that help us to grow.

The positive result of putting ourselves in the place of our fellow human beings is to feel what they feel, to understand their life's situations. Knowing that they are doing their best at their own level of creating their Life is the beginning of one of the highest energy vibrations we can realize: Empathy and Compassion.

Still your tongue and quiet your thoughts. Feel the Peace within you.

THERE IS NO VALUE, goodness, or humility in *not liking yourself.* Do not underestimate or judge yourself. Self-preoccupation -- whether egotistical and inflated or self-doubting and timid – limits your field of vision and your range of helpfulness. You diminish your Light and inner power by doing so.

Leave behind all fears and whatever hurt may be keeping you from rising to your highest potential. They tie you down and hold you back. In the Cosmic Chess Game of Life, we are constantly living through different Life experiences. Why choose to be a victim when you can triumph over darkness to reveal your glorious Light Being?

Many times, we become victims of our own thoughts and actions.

IT IS VALUABLE TO FEEL PAIN. Pain nourishes your courage. It can weaken the ego, strengthen humility, and increase compassion. Pain is a human process that we should not fight against. It's a lesson to let go of all attachment we may have. By living the experience of pain we mature and move forward.

THERE IS NO VALUE in using suffering as a badge of distinction, in playing the victim, or in believing that this manipulative attitude gives us the force to survive. Personalizing pain in suffering makes us lie to ourselves, ties us to the past, and limits our ability to live in the present. Life has pain and suffering. Buddhists believe that suffering is caused by ignorance and desire, and that by reducing desire, we reduce suffering. Suffering is a never-ending energy that keeps us enslaved, victimized by our own egos.

The solution to resolve suffering lies in restoring our natural state of love and happiness, by recreating a life of Peace and tranquility.

Since 1984, I have been searching for ways that my paintings may reflect the Light of God and the Light inside of each being. My work has been arduous, and I have often stumbled. I didn't lack for people who made fun of me and my "craziness." However, my Inner Being gave me direction and kept me firmly on the road to my passions and dreams of Life. One of them was to discover how to show the inner Light through invisible techniques in art. Impelled by a force beyond myself, I never gave up on my goal of portraying the Invisible World – to reveal the Divine Light that is found inside every one of us.

The vibrations emitted by my paintings and their crystals when exposed to the ultraviolet Light, represent much more than a certain technique or invisible colors. They are very high vibrations that move and elevate the viewer to higher and superior dimensions where the Spirit is manifested. Works of art that have a higher purpose, are created by our Spirits. Artists know they humbly become the *physical tools that the Spirit utilizes to show the Truth.*

I learned that there are multiple dimensions of color that vibrate and affect us in various ways. Within the Invisible world different spectra of colors vibrate. Our world would change instantly if we were seeing or living under the influence of infrared or ultraviolet vibrations or x-rays – or hearing or feeling in a different range of frequencies. In a world of enhanced ultraviolet, we would be able to transmute ourselves from brute, self-centered beings to radiant, Spiritual Beings. We would be seeing the world in an entirely different way.

At the other end of the spectrum, underneath the red color, the infrared frequencies bring our energy down to a world of infra-vibration, beneath what is human. An infra-human being belongs to a group lower than human beings and dwells in the lower red frequencies that ignite our animal, infernal side. Many people – through the psychic and physical violence born of hatred and anger – live "infra-human" lives. From this energy, people attract people and situations at the same or similar vibrational levels. As the principal law in homeopathy says, *like attracts like.*

We enter the dimension of Life – a scale of multiple vibrations of Consciousness and emotion. We are born into the physical world. When we open our human eyes, the eye of the Spirit closes. The Mastery of this Game of Life is to have both eyes open: to be awake in Life and not asleep to the reality of our Eternal Presence.

The first thing we do at birth is to breathe. We become inspired by Life – we inhale Life. To truly live is to live inspired, breathing every second as a reminder of who we really are. The beauty that Life offers us every day – the sun shining, the birds singing – brims over with delight, inspiring us. After our journey, consisting of diverse Life experiences and difficult tests, we die. Yet only the physical body dies. Our Soul is liberated and returns to its source of Light, taking with it the essence of all its learning experiences.

The universe and its Light conspire to give us what we emotionally and mentally desire. The tests that we face come to us with the same strength and design that are contained within ourselves. We receive only what we are able to support – no more, no less.

In the Invisible World, we find the answers to all of our doubts. When we discover our true reality, we begin to really know ourselves. All the feelings, emotions, and thoughts that create physical experiences are born in the

Invisible Dimensions. We do not see them, we cannot touch them, but we feel and think them.

In the Invisible World, we live in silence. In the sacred Heart of Light, our Spirit vibrates eternally.

What is the true world? Is it the world of illusion or the world of reality? Is it the physical world or the spiritual? How can we distinguish one from the other? How can we tell which is which?

Scientists are now discovering that our physical, material world is an "illusory world." Its frequency range and the way it operates depend on the perception of our sensory organs.

Every living creature perceives Life in a different way. Each person sees it through the lens of his or her own experience. We strive to validate what is in our mind's programming, our feelings, and our thoughts. Our sense of sight provides us with ninety percent of the information we receive. Without vision, we would perceive the world in a very different way. We would adapt to it differently. We would live only through hearing and the tactile senses. Our Invisible World, our intuition, and what is called the sixth sense would guide our Life.

The world is simply our perceived subjective reality. It is what exists within us and is projected into manifestation in our daily living.

Each of us experiences reality from the vibrations of his or her own Consciousness, as well as from the spiritual level that has been realized in our lives. This relates to what we call a "spiritual being." A low level of Consciousness gives us a low quality of spiritual life. A high level of Consciousness inspires us to higher actions, words, and feelings. It represents a higher spiritual awareness.

In the human experience, the Game of Life has to do with the union of both worlds: the visible and the Invisible – the body and the spirit. The body is the temple wherein the spirit takes temporary residence. Our spirit gives Energy to Life. It is, in turn, part of the great Energy of the Creator.

Nothing is separate or unrelated. The visible and Invisible worlds have their reasons for being. In both worlds, all beings have free will to experiment via Life's experiences according to their own intentions and actions. The idea that we are each unique, alone, and superior is central to the world of illusion. The Light and Our Spirits belong to the same world of Light. The only difference is between those who know it and work to reveal their Light, and those who live unaware of that reality.

As you play this game, you will learn invaluable lessons. You will learn that if you attack, you will be attacked. If you give, you will receive. *The boomerang effect* is set in motion. Just as with the boomerang, if you forcefully throw out an action, it will return to its origin with even greater force. Conforming to the Law of Attraction, it completes its mission through energy. It is inevitable. *What is sent out will come back.* Be just as careful with your thoughts, which are as big an energetic force as your actions!

Harmony is a path to Peace and a spiritual expression of joy and love.

If we ask for abundance with our thoughts, but our inner emotion tells us we don't deserve it, or that there is only so much to go around, what we attract will be various forms of lack.

The risk in this Game of Life is to lose the opportunity that Life gives us to grow and to expand our Light.

Reflections

Whether we are content just surviving or whether we want to really LIVE, we participate in Life as players and Creators. As a result, we will achieve success in our lives being winners. The good news about this "game" is that unlike any other game, the Game of Life invites everyone to win!

Competition has to do with a consciousness of limitation.

The goal of the *Cosmic Chess Game of Life* is to discover life's surprises. Acknowledge that life is an exciting journey. Ask yourself where your thoughts, actions, and choices will take you. We must free ourselves from our fears and worries and recognize our TRUTH. To do this, an honest look at how we are playing the game is essential.

Believe in Yourself. Always remember you are worth it. The deeper you love yourself, the more the universe will support you.

If we leave Life without asking people for forgiveness and without forgiving others – if we leave without resolving our karmic, emotional, or sentimental debts – if we leave without saying I LOVE YOU to the people we Love because we are afraid of being hurt – if we cause harm to others – and if we kill with physical weapons, or with the weapons of words by judging or speaking badly about our fellow man, then we will leave with a heavy weight, and our heart will not be Light. None of these experiences will allow us to rise to the Light. This energetic weight will oblige us to return as many times as it takes to live the same human experiences that we did not resolve, until we pass through the difficult challenges of all the tests put before us and finally learn the lessons of this and past lives.

The School of life is about learning, growing, expanding awareness, and doing so with joy, gratitude, and the realization of what a unique opportunity this is for us.

Many times we say, "It happened on its own," and "it came from out of the blue," wanted or not. If we commit an act of low vibration and experience negative consequences, it is our responsibility and no one else's. This energy will return to us unless we have the strength of character to admit our action, cleanse it, and with an open heart, humbly ask for forgiveness.

Happiness, Gratitude, Peace, and Love are the most important realities in the Cosmic Chess Game of Life.

We come from the dimension of Light in order to be born into a slower and heavier vibratory dimension: the material world. The body is the vehicle of our soul, allowing us to perfect it. When the body dies, the soul is liberated in order to re-enter the pure vibrations of the Light.

Saying: " I have the power to change my unwanted thoughts, feelings and emotions, from darkness and hatred into love, peace and light"... Helps you "program" a powerful state.

Choose your friends wisely; surround yourself with people who pull you up, instead of people who "drag you down." Choose people who are aware of your greatness.

Thus, when our time comes, the Angel will embrace us, we will then be lifted up and raised to the dimension of Supreme Light. Knowing that we did everything within our means to elevate ourselves, we recognize with joy the progress we have made in our Cosmic Chess Game of Life.

*C*reation evolves and constantly transforms itself. We must learn to use our creative forces to flow with this evolution and the changes that co-create our lives. Thus, we elevate ourselves to encounter the Light once again.

Turn your fears into courage. Where you find one thing, you find its opposite, for there are two poles. It is Law.

If you are afraid of the darkness, turn the other way and look to the Light. Ignorance is dispelled by knowledge. It is the eternal interplay between Light and Dark. Darkness is a powerful instrument for revealing Light. Every hidden test is a revelation ... an opportunity for us

You gain strength, courage, and confidence with every life experience you dare to face.

To Love ourselves and to Love others is the goal of the Cosmic Chess Game of Life.

To master ourselves we need to master our minds.

My Notes:

_____

_____

_____

_____

Storms of Life © 2004 Jacqueline Ripstein

Lesson VII

The Storms of Life©

*"Everything flows out and in; everything has its tides;
all things rise and fall; the pendulum-swing manifests in everything;
the measure of the swing to the right, is the measure of the swing
to the left; rhythm compensates"*
The Kybalion

The storms of Life stir our Souls.

To every action, there is always a reaction.

*Behind what is visible, there is always something Invisible that subtly
activates the material and visible experience.*

*In Life there is always an advance and a retreat, a high and a low,
a rising and a collapse.*

*There is an increase and a decrease of energy every second in
the universe.*

Our own thoughts can drown us.

The weight of anger, shot through with pain, can sink us.

Stress can drown us.

Life has its ups and downs, and both embrace a reward for us.

The ups give us high moments of Joy and Love.

The downs teach us the lessons that will strengthen us.

Lack of self-esteem restrains us.

Identifying with the ego misguides us completely.

Living in fear and darkness instead of Light weakens us.

Identifying with material things entraps us.

Identifying with only the material world obscures our true being.

Without health we lack the energy we need to survive.

Insensitivity to Love weakens us.

Sometimes storms come by themselves, but too often, it is we who create the storms in our lives...

We become vulnerable under the weight of beliefs instilled in us by others.

In the midst of life's storms, it can sometimes feel like everything has literally fallen apart.

But there is always a new beginning, to find hope, and rebirth after the devastation of any storm.

Waves in the ocean are stirred by an inner, invisible energy. Life is created from an invisible dimension. In a similar way, all of Life's tests are created by our own individual needs to learn and to grow, so that we may awaken to the true reality of our Light being. With the ups and downs of each wave, we awaken to our inner strength and animate our Spirit.

The lesson in this painting teaches us about life's storms and trials. To guide us in how to deal and learn from them is the goal of this lesson's enlightenment. Life's storms are diverse, could be: death, a divorce, physical or emotional abuse, betrayal by a friend, or large-scale tragedies such as tsunamis and war. Grieving is a personal and highly individual experience; it is a natural response to loss. Grief is the emotional suffering you feel when something or someone you love is taken from you. In our material world we deal with many losses that can cause grief: death of a beloved person or pet, divorce, loss of health, loss of a job, or of financial stability, loss of security, etc. Losing someone or something you love or care deeply about is very painful. You may experience all kinds of difficult emotions and it may feel like the pain and sadness you're experiencing will never let up. These are normal reactions to a significant loss, and there are healthy ways to cope with the pain that, in time, can renew you and permit you to move on. A new you will appear after every life storm.

It's important to recognize that many times we create our own storms, and that once we identify their deep causes, we can learn to deal with them. We must confront the challenges and use them for our growth.

When a storm approaches us, we begin to lose our center, often shifting into extreme thought patterns and their by-product, pain. A wide range of feelings and symptoms is common during the grieving process, when you are feeling shock, numbness, sadness, anger, guilt, anxiety, or fear, Taking care of yourself helps immeasurably in these stressful times.

Sometimes we become either too emotional or too intellectual to learn to transmute those patterns we need to obtain balance. To balance our lives at every opportunity is an essential process. We must revise our path so that we can endure any storm and cope with any hardship. By learning and growing with every step we take, we reveal our magnificent being.

Do you remember at least one time when you lived through a life storm? How did you confront it? Before a storm comes near, it usually warns us in some way that it is close by and that we must prepare. All storms challenge and change our lives. From the darkness we perceive the Light. Order is born from disorder; harmony emerges from chaos.

All ends create a beginning...

It is important to discern the differences among storms that come to help us grow. Some of them are out of our hands, such as death. Others we unconsciously create through our connections to lower emotions, fears, and lack of self Love.

After experiencing the storms that crash into our lives, we pass through various emotional stages. The pain is so profound that, in order to recuperate, we must undergo a process of purification. This process may be short or long, depending on how fully we are able to learn the lesson involved in it and to accept it. The first phase of the crisis is usually a refusal to accept the experience, followed by anger, guilt, depression, and feelings of helplessness in the face of an uncontrollable experience.

At some point in our life, we all deal with loss. Storms are not welcomed. The death of a loved one, the ending of a loving relationship, losing our health, suffering pain, disappointment, violence, hatred...any of this events can leave us stunned and in despair, but they are part of our life's journey. There are many kinds of grief, which affect us: personal, communal, even the deaths of people we've never met, such as Mother Teresa. We realize we have lost a compassionate human being who changed the lives of many.

How do you move on from grief?

First, let go, surrender to pain. Resistance creates more pain. Second, it's important to understand that any situation that creates pain in us has a learning side attached to it. As we go deep within ourselves to reveal our shadows, we can then connect to our Light to discover our lesson. This is part of our growth challenge.

In dealing with grief and sorrow, we find that everyone's grieving process is different. There are stages we need to pass through, and each person goes through his or her unique experience. As happens in digestion, for example, we eat, and then a process that is out of our control starts. The stages are connected to the inner feelings we had for the person who is the cause of our experience of loss. Some people may start with denial, some with anger. We then plead or bargain for a different outcome. We are humbled by our lack of joy and feelings of helplessness and exhaustion. We fall into long-term depression or live moments of melancholy and despair. Our Spirit connection is "low." Yet I implore you: know that all is okay! All stages are essential for our renewal. Living through the pain is as important as living the joy. It is how we deal with both, how well we accept life's tests without resistance, that will help us elevate our consciousness.

Resistance creates more pain.

The storms of Life serve as catalysts. With their energy they help us transform everything needed along the road to self-regeneration. They help us change our perception from one based in the physical world to that of the Spiritual world. Learning from them helps us shift from a world of chaos to a world of inner Peace.

In order to reach a world of Peace, we need first to find inner Peace within ourselves.

There are many types of storms in our lives, and all manifest in their own particular ways. Physically and emotionally, if we trust that we will learn from them, they lead to our awakening. Trials of Life manifest in myriad ways, such as sickness, death, loss, injustice, abuse, accidents, acts of crime, and all manner of adverse circumstances. During a "Life storm," we experience a constant beating and much confusion. It feels like the rising and falling of ferocious waves that are pushed by furious, unstoppable winds. They become more intense as the force grows. Violently and without mercy, the waves toss us about. Sometimes in the midst of a storm, other storms appear. "When it rains, it pours." Taking a double beating, we end up exhausted, worn out, and perhaps even humbled by the storms. Yet if we are open to changes in our lives and are willing to learn, the storms will have served their purpose.

The drive to survive – and even thrive – is activated within us, and we are forced to examine our static values, beliefs, and emotions. Our old structures are broken down, and the idea of who we believe we are has changed.

Although resentment, anger, and guilt no longer attach us to suffering in Life, we are afraid to let go of them. It is much like letting go of someone we thought we loved but who has only hurt us.

Without always realizing it, at the end of every trial or storm, we are fully alive. Not only are we still breathing, we are more conscious than before! We have been strengthened and subtly enlightened.

Faith, hope, and knowing that our Spirit is Eternal and that our Creator will take us by the hand without ever letting go strengthens our walk through Life. When we realize this, we see that the storm has indeed passed, that it now belongs to the past. In its wake come new hope and the strength to elevate our Consciousness to an expanded perception of our lives.

Years ago, when I was searching for new *Invisible techniques* in my art and going deeply into the study of colors on esoteric levels (that is, seeing colors beyond this physical plane and understanding how their frequencies affect us), I looked into their significance beyond matter and discovered that colors, like music, have endless octaves of vibration. My inner need to know more, to understand Life more deeply, led me to many unknown paths. Colors and emotions go hand in hand, they vibrate manifesting each other, and by understanding the colors that the body emanates through our "Aura" we could easily figure out the emotion it's deriving from. They go hand in hand; one mimics the other.

For me, colors are the Invisible vibrational language of the universe, and through them, we can come to know the hidden Truth within all life. Colors can reveal emotions, feelings, and thoughts as infinite secrets contained in the Universe.

Does sickness have a purpose? Why is cancer an internal war? What relationship does illness have with our feelings and emotions?

It has been shown that stress, rage, depression, sadness, loss of faith, etc., depress our immune system and are harmful to every cell. Our white cells contain the energy of Light within our bodies. When our Light, our Joy, Hope, or Love goes down, the body gets hit too, and immunity is depressed. A cancerous tumor resembles a dark dense mass; it's made of negative condensed energy.

I associated the white color of the cells of the immune system with the essence of the white color of Light. And I've reached the conclusion that when our Light dims in times of personal storms (bringing dark and muddied emotions in shades of gray, black, and brown), our immune system will also grow weak.

Even slightly disturbing emotions and thoughts negatively affect our health, making us more vulnerable to illness. Positive emotions benefit our health, inspiring us to rise above difficulties, bringing Light and restoring health. A smile, whether our own or someone else's, lifts our mood.

Thus I learned that the treatment of illness should take emotions into primary consideration. The body is not separate from its emotions; they are bonded energetically. I see all forms of Light as essential for healing. Therefore, all treatments that contain Light would, by their very nature, be healing. Cancer shows up as dark areas on X-rays. Light has the power to shine away darkness.

The colors that our bodies emanate give us a perfect view of the content of our emotions. These colors comprise what is called the *aura*. The energy that we put out is distinguished by an array of halo-like colors around our bodies that express different states – mental, emotional, and physical. Everything in the universe vibrates. Every atom, every electron in our bodies, our thoughts, and our feelings are vibrating. Hence, we may define the aura as the reflector of our energetic and emotional body. It contains information that is revealed through colors.

These chromatic vibrations in turn relate to all the energy that vibrates from Mother Nature, including her plants and animals. The world of nature is a symphony of color. The colors vibrate and connect on an Invisible level, creating a common language without words.

The universe, the planets of the solar system, and all Life on earth are connected by the same energy that manifests a language of colors – a silent language that vibrates and connects us to the primordial Light.

If we focus our mind on the Light, we will strengthen our immune system.

Our Life experiences have powerful reasons to be. When we leave painful wounds behind without healing them, Life returns them to us. For a wound to heal, Life will oblige us to go back to examine it. An emotional wound is like a physical wound – it must be treated and left to close and heal. Revisiting these wounds offers us the opportunity to reevaluate our lives and to heal the emotional pain and anger that have not been fully experienced and accepted. In "reevaluate," the embedded word "value" says it all – one needs to appreciate the value and strength in oneself in order to use the abundant opportunities to *"re-e-value-ate."*

Colors help us discover the hidden secrets of Life. They reveal our emotional states.

I painted *The Storms of Life* after a dream -- I should say a nightmare -- I had on December 5, 2004. There were huge waves; I saw them rolling toward land. The storms of life had been activated. The waves were destroying people, communities, everything; there was heartache, loss, tragedy, and pain. My dream was vivid and I was part of this great horror. I could hear people screaming, frantic to survive. I saw my own people drowning under the rage of the waves. I also clearly saw a father holding a baby up, trying to keep him from drowning, while he himself was drowning. There was great pain and suffering.

I could barely breathe and felt as if I were drowning, when I awoke, I took a large canvas and with great anxiety began to reproduce what I had seen in my nightmare. I painted for hours. I felt pain in every cell of my body; I needed to portray what was given to me in the dream. On the second day, with the painting still unfinished, I sent a message with the unfinished painting to various people, informing and warning them that a storm would soon arrive. When my daughter Stephanie, distressed by my dream, asked me where it would happen, I answered that I did not know.

On the 26th day of the same month, the Indonesian tsunami occurred, only 21 days after my nightmare.

The tragedy moved our humanity. The pain of one became the pain of all. The people of the whole world united to help the victims. Many thousands of people died.

I observed my painting after the tsunami. As I was finishing it, I got the chills. The painful memory made me realize that it is not only the personal storms that move us to change, but also the storms that touch us as a civilization and a shared humanity. A profound pain still reverberates through me as I recall that dream. I questioned myself: Because I had seen the vicious storm before it happened, did that mean it was a destined event? Were the people who died destined to die? One thing was for sure -- the storms of Life help us to reach new and more elevated states of consciousness.

We want to avoid the storms, but it is impossible to do so. Storms are always present, or on their way. Perhaps today we don't see them on the horizon, but they will arrive tomorrow. We have to learn to co-exist with emotional storms, to take advantage of their teachings, rather than try to avoid them. If we turn away in fear or anger, those emotions will pull them right back to us with even more strength.

Adversity will always exist; the best shelter is to find our Spirit's defense within us. In doing so, we will know that nothing can destroy us, that our **Spirit is Eternal,** that *"faith moves mountains."* In the eye of the hurricane one finds Peace. If the roots of the tree are strong, it will resist the storm, but if they are weak, the storm will pull it from the ground.

The universe, the suns, the worlds, man and animals, plants and minerals, the forces and the energy, the mind and the material all manifest the rhythm of Life. Each entity in its own way expresses the creation and destruction of worlds, the alpha and the omega of a Life cycle, the rise and fall of nations, the cycle of Life and death, and finally, the mental and emotional state of the human being.

Experiences such as the death of loved ones, physical and emotional pain, hatred, frustration, deception, betrayal, guilt, abandonment, and exhaustion are among the many challenges that tempt us to give up and lose faith. What beats us down is the belief that we are destroyed. Our own thoughts destroy us.

And yet, the end of one chapter is always the beginning of a new one. After nighttime, comes the day. What does it mean to be awake? Does it mean to open one's eyes and start the day on auto-pilot? No! When we simply fall into an automatic operating system that is connected to the material world, we are still fast asleep, no matter how efficiently we operate. To be awake means to open our eyes and acknowledge our Invisible World – our Spirit. It means knowing that we are co-creators of our lives. It means to acknowledge our union with everything. It means to accept that within our bodies there is a Light Being that gives us the privilege and the reason to live.

How should we confront conflicts? Conflicts produce disharmony, bringing disequilibrium that derails our body and mind. They generate more pain and disharmony if we resist, deny, or ignore our emotions and feelings. Resistance to pain generates more pain. The fear that we have when we think of change can paralyze us. Moving to unknown places or getting in unfamiliar situations can excite fear in us, and fear weakens us more. It is the lack of true knowledge that obscures our vision.

The key is to take responsibility for our lives without blaming anybody. It is to find within us the solutions that can give us Peace.

Peace comes in learning to balance our lives, to balance the yin and yang energies, the male and female energy within us, and to recognize our Light, our darkness, and our inner strength.

How can anyone value us if we don't value ourselves?

As we look back, many painful Life experiences are now nothing but stories, yet we still give them the power to drown us.

We have a clear-cut choice about suffering. When we have a painful experience, like losing someone we love, there is a natural process for us to follow. If we do not resist this process, we eventually flow into a healing state.

Each challenge gives us the option to change our Consciousness or attitude, which means we do not stay where we were before. Focusing on what we lack, and on suffering, anger, and greed can hold us under the churning waters.

Many storms do not come from our external world; they come from our internal thoughts, feelings, noise, outside influences, or pain, and are constantly stirred and nourished by the ego system. Moved by these internal waves, we create them! The ego has multiple ways to control us, to claim us as its own. One of them is guilt. Guilt, like many of our other ego shadows, tortures us. We use it to torture ourselves. To free ourselves from guilt, we need to learn to let go of our self-criticism by replacing it with self-forgiveness and acceptance. Guilt serves the ego with forces of darkness, keeping us far away from a state of inner Peace.

Guilt drowns us and prevents us from being connected to our Light.

Too often we attach ourselves to the past – to pain, to anger, to guilt – by reliving the "stories" of our lives. I invite you to look back and see that those past experiences are now nothing more than stories.

How many times have we admitted that we feel like we are drowning in our own thoughts? We don't need external storms or earthquakes to feel this

way. We often cause these feelings ourselves, and we feed them without realizing it.

Did you know that an eagle anticipates storms and reacts before they appear? Sensing that the storm is drawing near, the eagle will fly to a higher place to await the winds. When the storm whips through, the eagle spreads its wings in a position such that the wind pushes them, lifting the eagle above the storm. As the storm crashes upon those who are downing below, the eagle soars above it.

The eagle does not escape the storm; it beats it by using the storm to elevate itself.

Reflections

Guilt drowns us, preventing us from being connected to our Light!

Understanding that there is a cause for every effect and an effect for every cause helps us deal with our actions.

We attach ourselves to the past, to pain, to anger, to guilt, by reliving the STORIES of our lives. I invite you to look back, observe, and see. Those old experiences are now only stories.

Take care to create neither outer nor inner storms. We create outer storms by joining in fights, inflicting hurt and pain onto others. We create inner storms when we unleash our egos and when our thoughts and emotions are out of control.

Grief is a process that takes time. It is important to live through it, because as we resist it, it creates more pain. We must remember that behind all darkness there is always Light. As we face the loss, we undergo a metamorphosis; we come out of the experience renewed, reborn into a state where we have attained spiritual knowledge or insight, which will enlighten our lives.

Prepare yourself by fortifying your Inner Being to resist adversity.

All storms contain within them something positive to learn from. They can cleanse our darkness and shine our Spirit, remove us from lower vibrations or people, and unite people.

Most of the time when we try to interpret the silence or words of other people, we base our interpretation on our own Life experiences, including those connected to pain and low self-esteem. What others say or don't say has little to do with us.

Pain is inevitable. But suffering is a heavy anchor that holds us back from a sea of joy!

As we balance our lives, we reconnect to the Light; we live with Lightness and Joy; we smile, sing, and play. Our lives become ... lighter!

The Arts are a powerful means of releasing pain, anger, and stress. I invite you to start practicing any form of art you like. Being good at it -- or not -- is not the goal; through moments of inspiration, you'll connect to your soul.

Nothing prevents us from focusing our attention in the direction of what we most desire, to change a depressing thought to one of joy.

See reality without distortion, without interpretations or judgments. Be tolerant and be patient with yourself and others.

Love Life. Preserve your inner Peace without handing it over to any situation or person.

Respect Mother Earth and all her children, her animals, all life within her. Any harm we create will eventually come back to us or to our future generations, and more powerfully than when it first "went out!"

We must ask ourselves how a storm can be our ally, how it can open the way to changes in our lives that further our growth. Its energy can help us cleanse our lives by forcing us to leave behind what is no longer useful.

Our goal in Life is to express our inner Being, our Light.

In the presence of devastating storms, there are some people who look at the storm and see only its darkness. They become weak ... they tremble. Others focus on the Light through the storm and find themselves in search of hope. They are the ones who have not lost trust and who know that if they look to the Light, all things possible can be found in the Light itself.

Feel your heart full of joy, faith, and hope.

*W*hen a storm seems to break us, it destroys the trivial things and the fears appear. It offers us the opportunity to recreate ourselves, to open ourselves to a greater capacity for Light than we had before.

The more significant is the loss, the more intense is our grief. Life is a present, a gift. As such may only be celebrated and appreciated. When suffering unnecessarily, the ego keeps darkening our light.

To change our mental state we must change our vibration and learn to balance our lives. By correcting even the slightest degree of negative vibration, we shift our energy. In order to heal it is necessary to face grief and actively deal with it.

Search for and embrace the positive side of your storms. Life isn't only about how to survive the storm, but how to dance in the rain!

Focus on Love and not on hate – or even on mild distaste. Feel within you the vibration of Love.

Life is not about how I fall and get stuck on the ground, but how I rise up from every fall.

Acceptance is... When I'm at peace with what has happened.

My Notes:

_____

_____

_____

_____

Confusion © 1977 Jacqueline Ripstein

Lesson VIII

Confusion©

According to the Book of Genesis in the Old Testament:
"When man wanted to reach Heaven God confused their language."
God wanted to punish mankind for its arrogance in building
the Tower of Babel to get to Heaven.

Why do we continue speaking various languages without
understanding each other?

Is it the language that separates us?

Or is it the lack of understanding among us, and our false beliefs?
We are all human beings on the journey of Life.

The ego traps us into believing that we have supremacy.

The material World triggers confusion in us, while the Spiritual reality
triggers the Truth within us.

The ego system dwells in and feeds on confusion.

Once we conquer chaos, a state of Inner Peace prevails.

$\mathcal{W}$hat is confusion? It is a state of disorder, disharmony, chaos, and agitation. In confusion, we are concealed by the veils of the ego. In confusion, the shadows cover our Light, impede our ability to see the Light, and drag us toward the labyrinths that descend to the core of darkness.

This lesson will help us disentangle ourselves from old thought patterns, from the past as individuals and as humanity. It will take us on a journey into clarity and consciousness. Beliefs are inputted into our belief system; they are not necessarily ours to being with; they belong to a "program" that is running our lives. To open that program and discard what we don't accept and to discern what part of it belongs to the Truth of our Spirit is a job for consciousness. As you discover what has trapped you, you learn how to balance your life, to create order where there is chaos. You can do this by becoming aware of your creative powers, by taking responsibility for all of your actions, by understanding that separation starts with a thought which turns into a belief and then creates a reality. Humans think they are separated from other human beings, but a drop of the ocean belongs to the same ocean, and a human being is a fragment of humanity. By discovering and applying the power of your inner-self, you take a real role in reconstructing your life.

Confusion is a symptom of being trapped in a non-reality dimension. Confusion depicts a state of chaos, of disorder, a lack of balance.

The opposite of being confused is to be clear, balanced, and enlightened.

Why are there wars? And why do we try to subjugate, change, kill, and convert others? Wanting to impose our beliefs on others and conquer other human Beings is arrogant.

When we try to demonstrate that we know more than others, to show them we are superior, we conquer them. When we judge others in order to put them down and control them, our egos have taken over and their roots have dug deep into our own hearts.

We are an essential key to the growth of society and civilization. We are active human Beings, influencing every person in our particular society with whom we come in contact. Many times our actions affect others we don't even know. Each action we take has a multiplying effect, but to complete its energy cycle, this energy always ends up coming back to us. All of our actions affect our environment. We run our lives through diverse programs installed in our minds, most of which we are not aware of.

Each one of us contains a grain of the sand necessary to create a world of Peace and Love. Giving to others and not taking from them is our main task.

When we are not in contact with our Light, we hand over command to the darkness inside of us. The ego becomes delighted when we ignore our strength and allow our weakness to grow. Confusion takes over. We give up our inner-power.

Our Life's main lesson is to transmute from being trapped in the reign of shadows to discovering and revealing our Light.

Guilt is a betrayal of ourselves. It is the path to sabotaging our lives. Guilt is a way of torturing ourselves constantly. To heal it, we need to learn to let go of our self-criticism and replace it with acceptance and self-forgiveness.

Guilt serves the ego keeping us far from our inner Peace and our Light!

Guilt anchors us and prevents us from connecting to our Light! Guilt creates confusion. Arrogance entails pride. Greed nourishes vanity, conceit, impertinence, and pedanticism. All of these traits guarantee more living in confusion.

When we start unveiling our egos and confront and eliminate our arrogance, our majestic, magnificent being appears. As confusion vanishes, clarity starts to empower us.

When the "Tower of Babel" collapses, the ego of humanity will collapse with it.

When we are conceited, we lose humility. Vanity, pride, arrogance, haughtiness, self-conceit, self-love, self-satisfaction, self-glorification, narcissism, egotism, pretension, ostentation – all these states of low vibration confuse us; they take us far away from our true worth. We lose track of who the Creator is and who is the created.

In my painting *"Confusion"* here in this lesson, the man at the center of the picture reminds us: "Centuries have passed and we continue speaking various languages without understanding each other, without achieving Peace."

He whispers: "What's happening? Why haven't we advanced? Why do we continue to kill one another? Why do we still not understand each other? Why are we the same as before?

Where do we encounter confusion? Why don't we see with clarity? What blocks our path?"

As humanity, we have been up and down. Each civilization and generation forms its own identity, carrying on the legacy of knowledge from the last one. On the evolutionary scale, cavemen were the closest to the animal state. They represented the lowest vibration of a Consciousness that was in the process of elevating itself in order to ascend to the next state of Being. Survival was the motor of their lives.

Just as each of us faces tests, humanity as a group also experiences tests. Through these tests we have the capacity to elevate ourselves individually, as a society, and as a civilization. We have the power to create new generations with greater inner strength that is closer to our Spiritual Truth.

The history of humanity shows us that times of war, atrocities, and turbulence bring changes in societies. It is important to understand that in every moment every creature is living in a constant process and that everything that happens is not by chance. The process of awakening starts within ourselves. It then flows from one person to another, from one generation to the next.

Does barbaric genocide occur with no explanation? Why do certain generations or certain communities suffer more than others? Why do tsunamis, huge fires, earthquakes, storms, and floods destroy so many innocent people, animals, and nature itself? Why do these things recur at different moments in the course of human history?

I ask myself the following: Does this all have to do with the continuing tendency of humanity to cleanse itself through pain in order to create the birth of new and more awakened generations?

Is it possible that by witnessing tragedy, pain, famine, and destruction, past generations have learned new forms of survival? Now, is our civilization ready to reveal more compassion for all Life on the planet Earth? Perhaps these situations once again will turn into a tool to reveal the Light.

Sometimes farmers, or Earth itself, cause fires with the purpose of renewing the Earth in order to increase agricultural production or to renew ecosystems.

Freud explored the depth of the mind where one shelters emotions that rule one's Life. This exploration contributed to further research into Consciousness leading to the later recognition that the power of the mind is infinite with the capacity to be both creative and destructive at the same time.

Our thoughts contain the seeds that create all of our experiences.

One person is representative of humanity as a whole. One by one we can create change. Thus, as the revelation appears in the middle of chaos and confusion, humanity will come out the victor, overcoming all storms and suffering, while advancing towards the Light.

We are now living through unique times of change. We have walked down many roads together; we have opened doors to new ideologies and technological advances. We have suffered and cried, laughed and rejoiced together, but the time has come to reveal who we really are: to stop acting and using masks, to stop hiding in the darkness, to recognize that the power of our mind is infinite and creative and that with this power we can Create and destroy. We can discover that our thoughts contain the seeds that grow and become all of our experiences. The time has come to finally reveal our inner Light!

Our Present world as we know it is collapsing. Are you ready to recreate and renew yourself as an individual and as an integral part of your civilization?

Are you ready to let go of beliefs that are not part of your true essence? The moment of change has come. Our hidden powers are now being stimulated by higher vibrations, helping us to raise our Consciousness. We have to start by taking responsibility for who we are and for what we have created. The moment of humanity's awakening is dawning.

Since the international monetary catastrophe of the material world, which we erroneously believed was so secure; we have arrived at a continuously deepening abyss. Everything happens for a reason. For even as we fall, the chasm allows us to see bright sparkles of Light that little by little show us that our Spirit has nothing to do with this material world.

The spiritual world hides behind the material world, just as the Soul hides within the human Being.

Ask yourself if there are experiences from the past that continue to be active in your Present Life. If yes, you can't delete them, but by becoming Aware of not repeating that suffering again, one can overcome them.

Search within; discover your fears one by one. In the end, your fears are yours alone. You can replace them with courage and confidence. This will strengthen the connections with your inner Being. As we recover our inner strength, Life will flow more freely.

Accept your Spiritual reality; the Light always shines within you.

Sometimes we can't see the sun ... it is covered by layers of dark clouds. The Soul as well is always shining within us. Even though we can cover it with clouds of anger, fear, resentment, it is a matter of focusing beyond the dark clouds and being certain that the Light will not fail to shine.

We are already becoming more aware of our hidden powers – making ourselves responsible for all consequences of our actions. The moment has come in which humanity needs to wake up from its deep sleep.

The moment of the revelation of our Invisible World has come.

It has taken us eons to get to the point where we are now. The change that we are experiencing is very subtle and is being manifested in different forms. Tired of wars, we begin to protest. Our safety is falling into a delicate situation. Our freedom is being compromised. We are starting to see sparkles of the Light. Our need for Truth has been ignited. We are discovering that Unity is strength, while separation is weakness. Our constant search has shown us that the answers are not outside of us in the material world, but within us. At the end of our Life, material objects remain behind and we take with us only our actions and their consequences. Only the Love that we were able to share will remain forever. Love vibrations can never be destroyed.

Are we separated by different languages or merely the belief that we are separated? Our thought processes make us think that we are different, but we are all human Beings, aren't we? And there is only One Light that created all of us!

How much are we affected by the universe that is in continuous movement? The planets take a step nearer to and farther from the Earth. Every movement we make creates a change in our Universe. Every star that shines, moves, or dies, affects our lives as well. We are energetic beings with a great capacity to capture energies continuously. We transmit and receive. We are part of a whole energy system. Certain types of energy affect us by making us weak and certain energies lift us up. The Universe continuously vibrates and emits vibrations that we receive without realizing it.

When we create a short circuit in our system, we manifest that short circuit in the lives of others, and throughout the whole Universe.

Life today is accelerating as a result of the high vibrations that we receive every second. Time is speeding up with this increase of energy. The most recent changes have included the false belief that the world was going to end in 2012. There is no end. We are already living through these changes; we are experiencing events, catastrophes, and events that have never happened before. The changes are showing us that we are not in control, that the world we thought we knew is not as we thought. The true changes will take place within ourselves, as we shift our perception and awaken from a dormant state, discovering our Light and manifesting a time of Enlightenment.

With this opening we will begin to ascend to higher levels of Consciousness. New realities are already being born as a consequence of the collapse of the material world. Many we can't see. A unity with Heaven is being created every second. As we uncover the Light within us, all heavenly Beings will soon be revealed. Little by little, lesson-by-lesson, change has brought us to this time of Enlightenment. We are now nearing a new space where we are obliged to achieve a balanced state: equilibrium between our material world and our Spiritual reality, a balance between our visible and our Invisible World. This balance is in our own body, mind, and Consciousness.

The illusionary world nurtures confusion, while balance creates clarity.

Confusion births chaos.

All struggles are born from lack of knowledge between our material world and our Spiritual world.

Beliefs of false identities create in us confusion.

Confusion is defined as a lack of understanding. Confusion can be due to a mental confusion status, injuries, shock, disorientation, and memory loss. People who have experienced emotional trauma, physical violence, domestic abuse, anxiety, depression and other psychological issues can benefit from expressing themselves creatively. Great breakthroughs can emerge after times of dissolution, chaos, and confusion.

The American Art Therapy Association describes art therapy as "a mental health profession that uses the creative process of art making to improve and enhance the physical, mental and emotional well-being of individuals of all ages. It is based on the belief that the creative process involved in artistic self-expression helps people to resolve conflicts and problems, develop interpersonal skills, manage behavior, reduce stress, increase self-esteem and self-awareness, and achieve insight."

The Arts are a creative and Spiritual expression that for centuries have narrated the history of humanity. All civilizations have been nurtured by the manifestation and expression of this creative and superior Being living within each of us. The Arts inspire our Beings, nurture hope and activate the Light within us ... they are the language of our Soul.

In order to be part of the New Age, we must re-invent ourselves, propel our creative forces, and re-activate our right brain, which is connected to our artistic essence. Any journey contains an essential place where creativity can help to innovate and re-create. Our right brain is the portal to our Freedom and inner Peace.

The Arts are the portals that connect us to our freedom, our Light, our Spirit ... a sparkle of the Light of our Creator.

As the co-creator of your Life, ask yourself: What experiences do I want to change from the past? What dreams do I want to manifest as a reality? It is possible to change all programming; it just takes guts, action, awareness and responsibility. Remember that it is your thoughts that tie you down and anchor you to the past. Let these thoughts go and free yourself!

Check your connections to your Inner Being. See how you can strengthen them. Raise your self-esteem by accepting and appreciating that you were created as unique and magnificent. Look ahead at the challenges facing you. Create a conscious union with your Spirit and let this be your guide. Rejoice in your Light and remember that the Light in you shines always. When new possibilities open, your fears will become weaker.

Reflections

What have we learned from our past as individuals and as a civilization?

Revise, restructure your belief system. Every belief, every identity we have acts as a powerful resistance to true awareness, veiling our true being.

Live the awakening, the renewal, the Life, the flow. No second that passes is ever repeated.

Faith moves mountains. Faith together with Hope forms the force that keeps us afloat through the big tests of Life.

Why do we speak various languages and continue not to understand that there is only one internal language that represents the Truth? Is there a silent language we can all speak that would be understood from heart to heart? *A language of Love?*

Discover your Truth; reveal your Light.

Your thoughts create vibrations, and those vibrations manifest your desires. Be careful of what you are thinking!

We attach ourselves to the past, to pain, to anger, and to guilt by reliving the "Stories" of our lives. I invite you to look back and see ... those past experiences are now only stories ... but they have become programs that rule our minds.

Is the confusion we are all living internal or external?

After we master our inner confusion, we awaken to our true identity.

Our present world is collapsing. Are you ready to let go, to recreate and renew yourself?

Check your connections to your Inner Being. See how you can strengthen them. Raise your self-esteem, knowing that you were created unique and magnificent.

Awakening entails seeing that external forces control us and drag us down roads that are not desirable. To awaken is to listen to our inner voice, the voice that guides us on the road to inner – and outer – freedom. It is to follow our intuition as we are guided through our trials and through darkness, knowing that the awakening of our humanity is in our hands.

We are the legacy of a humanity that is the product of thousands of experiences from myriad, past civilizations. The tests they have faced and the progress they have made are the teachings we needed for the awakening process. Through what we are all creating now as a present civilization we are placing down the foundations for the future of succeeding civilizations. Do not go through the effort of awakening only for yourself; do it for your children, and their children's children.

Together, we can manifest a world of Peace and Love and leave this as a legacy for future generations.

We must learn from older lessons instead of repeating them.

It takes valor to recognize we had a fall in life,
and it takes more courage to stand up again!

*A*waken to the possibility of creating a true change in your life. Make yourself responsible for this change. Create your destiny. Take the hand of other human Beings because the change that can be achieved together will have a greater impact.

Identities confuse us.

Confusion is chaos, noise, disorder, and war. Peace is the reflection of inner order, stillness, Harmony.

Remember that creative forces and your imagination are your most powerful weapons. Utilize them. Focus your attention and begin to activate what you desire. Feed this purpose with your Faith. Feel this intention in your heart and use your imagination to visualize your desires.

As you awaken and create your shift to awareness, you are then helping manifest the awakening of a new humanity.

Activate your inner strength, manifest freedom, and arm yourself with Love and Compassion. Vibrating at these levels, nobody will be able to harm you.

My Notes:

_____

_____

_____

_____

The Jail of the Ego © 2009 Jacqueline Ripstein

Lesson IX

The Jail of the Ego©

"The real opposition is that between the ego-bound man, whose existence is structured by the principle of having, and the free man, who has overcome his egocentricity."
Erich Fromm

The most subtle shadow is that of the ego... If you think you've escaped it, look up -- it is sitting on top of your head!

Temptation *traps me...*

Greed blinds me...

Wealth *fools me...*

Vanity *nourishes my arrogance...*

Pride *makes me feel superior...*

Selfishness *beats me...*

Bitterness *poisons me...*

Envy *eats me up inside...*

Pain *restricts me...*

Humiliation *makes me feel like a victim...*

Revenge *gives me the illusion of strength...*

Anger *takes me out of control...*

Fear *controls me...*

hese are some of the shadow warriors in the army of the ego. When they capture us, the strength of our ego is reinforced and the connection to our Spirit is weakened.

This lesson is an essential learning tool for defeating our own shadows so that our Light may shine through. Our egos trap us in the world of illusion. Appearing to be us, they give us false identities and a false sense of self-worth. As we understand more about the function of our egos, the easier it becomes to take control, instead of letting ego control our lives. While it is impossible to destroy the ego system, we can use the shadows to reveal our Light. First we have to learn to identify the shadows within us; then we can rise above them, using them in our ascending journey.

This is not an easy lesson, so be aware that you may find it boring or start to feel sleepy. There can be much inner resistance from your ego to prevent you from discovering the Truth.

What is the ego? Ego is every emotion, feeling, or thought of low vibration that traps us in our smallness. The ego has numerous shadows, which gather and multiply; they blind and deceive us. Eventually they become so opaque we cannot see the Light. As we nourish the ego, it rejoices and grows stronger.

We give it our freedom. We give it control over our lives. It makes us feel -- amidst persistent doubt and dread -- superior and special, richer or perhaps smarter or better looking than others. It subtly places us in its envelope.

The man in this painting is saying: *"I am trapped in a cage which I built myself from pure gold; its brilliance mesmerizes me. Excuse me, but I'm very busy and have no time to talk. If I get distracted I may lose out on making more gold."* Is this his Spirit talking, or his busy ego? His cage is open; he could leave at any time. But he is transfixed by the shine of the reflected light.

Does this sound familiar to you? We get trapped; we are so busy in this material world that it feels impossible to stop what we are doing. So much stress and noise keep us far from our inner Peace. This lower state of Consciousness entraps us with its many shadow warriors, attracting to us people who move in the same low vibration. We then share our lives with those who vibrate like us.

And ...while we admire the gold's shine and are held transfixed by its outward allure, the seconds, the hours, and our entire lives pass before our eyes!

The rose opened her petals to the sun; she blossomed to give us her beauty and perfume, and then she died...Did we pause for a second of our Life to smell and admire her?

To remove our shadows, we must first identify them. But just as snake venom contains the power of a cure, so too is ego a powerful tool in revealing our Light. Overcoming the ego begins when we start to see beyond self-interest, when we open up our lives to share with and help other people.

Black holes in the Universe feed off stars of light. Many people connect to their darkness, just as those in the egocentric state feed off others in order to survive. They are called the "Vampire's of Light." By contrast, the Light shares, gives, nurtures.

The words *egoism, egocentric, egoistic, egomaniac --all contain the root word "ego"; the function of the ego* is to keep us in a *hypnotic state.* Any word that starts with -ego refers to a low-vibrational state of being. Thus limited, one focuses upon oneself and personal happenings as the primary view. Excessive fixation with oneself, referred to as selfishness, limits our giving to others. Commensurately, it limits our ability to receive Love from others!

One low state attracts another, creating a chain of similar vibrations. Fed by ego, shadows nourish the tedious and ugly dynamics of ingratitude, voracity, malice, and greed, among other odious qualities. Lack of gratitude is especially conspicuous, as it includes a lack of interest in those surrounding us.

***The egocentric state keeps us so self-absorbed that it puts us,
and very often others, to sleep.***

This state keeps us boringly self-centered, in a state of forgetfulness and obliviousness. The egocentric being is thus limited in his capacities to see beyond himself. Blind to the Light within, he can see Life only through the distortions of his shadows. To be asleep is a term I am using to show the numbness and blindness to life. Focusing in the present moment --which is all there really is -- is the abode of our Spirit in this lifetime. To awaken means, for starters, that we are aware that we are more than a material body. Our journey to finding our true essence, our Divine Being, begins to unfold when we awaken to the Spirit of God within.

The ego is an energy that feeds on both Light and weakness in order to exist; it is the creator of the world of duality, of the maya or illusion. Enslaved by the ego, we waste most of our energy focused in the shadows. To rise above it, we need to watch ego carefully in all its many guises within ourselves. A transformation takes place as we become increasingly aware ---revealing our great inner potential. When we experience rebirth, our true Being of Light is revealed. The ego, with all of its shadows, is therefore an essential energy, inspiring growth toward Consciousness. Of course, we can never entirely rid ourselves of ego and still remain discrete entities. Without its shadows, the opportunity and incentive to grow would not arise in the School of Life.

It takes a lot of courage to face our shadows. One must accept their presence, not fight them off. Once we spot our shadow (or weak spot), then we can transmute it by focusing on its opposite side: our strengths, our Light. We are learning that negative thoughts trap us in lower levels of negative vibrations. By elevating these dark feelings and thoughts, we can then shine Light into the darkness.

Our inflated ego seduces us and traps us into denser and lower dimensions. As we stop blaming others, while also recognizing that we're responsible for what we create and attract into our lives, we then become the *masters of our own lives.*

Ego is the linchpin to our earthly identity. Whether blatantly or covertly, the ego of most people reigns supreme. According to our experiences of growth or degradation, we identify and create with a personal image; we attach ourselves to a very particular identity. The control of the ego produces this attachment to the multiple masks with which we identify. We believe these fake identities define who we are. We ascribe "I" to our various roles: I'm an accountant, I'm a doctor, I am a mom, etc. All of these are roles and ego personalities, not the true Spiritual Being within us. As actors we play multiple roles. In actuality, we are only acting out these roles. The true inner Self is at one with our Spirit.

Light, on the other hand, spreads and creates more Light. It nourishes us with Peace, compassion, self-sacrifice, altruism, solidarity, and Love. It inspires us and gives us clarity. It shines away darkness and dispels the gloom, showing everything as it is. To be a Being of Light is to live in a state of clarity, taking full responsibility for our actions and our lives. This is our natural state of illumination.

As we unload our darkness, we become lighter...walking through Life with fewer burdens, lighter loads, and flowing with less and less resistance.

Our true Life mission is to acknowledge Love within ourselves and to shine the Light of our Creator.

When we give away our free will, we become blind slaves to the ego, without even being aware of it. As we surrender our inner power to the ego, our own shadows gather, darkening our world and leaving us depressed. In doing this, we unwittingly allow the darkness of the ego to diminish our Light energy. A never-ending story, the multiple shades of grey surround us as they slowly extinguish the colors of our Light. We are used to, and are surrounded by, a world that constantly feeds negativity. We grow accustomed to an over-abundance of negative news and become exploited by the media -- yet another negative dynamic. We're constantly urged to focus on the negative side of life. We have been programmed to give more of our focus and interest to the negative vibrations than to the positive. Low vibrations emanate from people whose thoughts and actions create a life of suffering, aggression, and victimization. They therefore attract others who vibrate at the same level of Consciousness as they, in turn surrounding themselves with accomplices who reinforce their lower emotions and actions.

When we focus our energy on the shadows, more and more negative thoughts, actions, and events are attracted into our lives.

The ego debilitates us. To unmask the ego, we must first analyze into ourselves and try to catch it in its most flagrant action. We need to understand that suffering, sadness, anger, and the inability to enjoy and appreciate are manifested and nourished by our complex ego system.

To realize transformation, we must confront ourselves, question our thoughts, and accept that every aspect of our lives is the result of what we are creating. By blaming others, we are just fooling ourselves. When we are able to go within, we can start cleansing our lives, controlling our thoughts and our tongues, being more aware of all the actions we take, and accepting full responsibility for our lives. This is the moment of metamorphosis, a moment that reveals our great potential and magnificence. The revelation of the biggest secret happens the moment we accept that we are beings of Light.

We contain within us both the ego with its shadows and the Being of Light. *Which one do you choose to be?*

The ego is essential for the growth of our Consciousness, since without its shadows, we would lack the contrast needed to see our Light.

Light and darkness are necessary forces in all of existence. To balance them out is Life's greatest challenge and opportunity.

The ego is expressed by the *"I,"* while in the Soul's reality, everything that exists is the *"AM."* The *"WE"* is where we know no separation.

The *"I"* connects us to our personality and identity, causing us to fall into egotism, while the *"I AM"* connects the body directly with our Spirit. All material life traps us in the world of illusion, causing us to become "self-centered" and to abide in an egotistical mode. The ego emphasizes our faults, our fears, and our grandiose notions about ourselves that are intended to counter those faults and fears. Our true talents, our Light, and our virtues represent a serious threat to the ego system, which insists upon taking full credit for those talents, and/or no responsibility at all for "unlucky" circumstances. Our Creative Forces are a gateway to our freedom from the world of illusion. Our right brain is the direct portal to that freedom, that Light.

Those who have found their center, their Light, are those who, through their creative forces, have inspired our lives, providing us beacons of inspiration that facilitate our own discovery of the Truth within. Once a human being "awakens," his or her very presence in the world serves to awaken others. The ego cannot stop this process.

"One candle can light thousands of candles, and the life of that candle will not be diminished." – The Buddha

All of our difficult experiences are specially designed for us to be able to see through them and to learn from them. They are designed from the same level of Consciousness that we inhabit. If we are at a first-grade level, our tests will be at that level only.

We develop a personality of the image we have chosen to create.

Complicit with the ego, we devise multiple masks that we identify with. Each serves to hide our flaws. When we believe that we are these personalities, and we identify with the roles we are playing, it can take quite a while before we realize that we are only acting. The only true identity we have is that of our inner Being — our Spirit.

I wear a mask to fool others so they don't see who I really am,
but the only one I fool is me...

We are constantly surrounding ourselves with excitement and noise; amid such chaos we cannot see our inner Being. We remain busy and entertained, and we are more "taken by" the darkness — and used to perceiving it — than we are receptive to the Light.

When we see a painting that depicts a particularly striking devil-being -as in some of the Tibetan mandala paintings done purposely to bring to the surface those evil egos — we find that identifying with our ego patterns is a smooth and automatic process. What we see and identify with reflects what is contained within us. Wrathful "deities" represent identification with negative thoughts, actions, and feelings. They embody all the inner afflictions, which darken our thoughts, our words, and our deeds.

When we are able to recognize the evil in others, we are actually seeing aspects of ourselves.

All negativity that we see in others helps us to realize our own, step by step, by increasing degrees of awareness; we then start achieving states of enlightenment. I know it's not easy to accept that when "we" fight, our negativity activates; by not recognizing our fighting mode, our ego is activated. The Truth is we cannot recognize anything outside of ourselves that is not also within our own ego system.

The encouraging news is that the moment we judge others presents a golden opportunity to pay attention. I invite you to take a look at the hand that you are using to judge someone as an idiot; I invite you to look for the idiot who hurled that judgment. ***Nothing exists outside of us that we are able to recognize, which we don't also harbor within ourselves. If we are able to pinpoint something, it is because we are familiar with its existence.*** Be careful about what and whom you judge, since you silently and invisibly reflect whatever vibrates inside of yourself.

We doubt our own Light and many times we are surprised by it. Meanwhile, we grow accustomed to accepting our negativity. Having it seems part of our necessity, our identity, and sleeping placidly or angrily in its bed, we curl up with it. We get hooked on the low vibrations of our shadows. This dependence – such as on drugs, alcohol, and overeating -- is difficult, but not impossible, to let go of.

The day we *"wake up"* and realize that we have been asleep, and that our days were devoted to a world of material delusions, we will see that these delusions obscure our true nature. But through constant spiritual practice they can be transformed into the wisdom of Clarity.

The delusion of ignorance becomes the wisdom of reality, and when we are able to realize this, we will cry out, with all of our hearts, *"No More!"* In this instant we are truly "born again." Our Consciousness expands, and we embark on our true-life journey: to awaken and to live through the guidance of the Light Being within us.

We forget who we really are because we are continuously being seduced by the ego system. The delusion of attachment traps us in a material world and makes us think we are merely the body, rather than the Soul that gives us Life. When we become aware and start turning things around, we tap into the wisdom of discernment.

The drunkard in the bar is fascinated with alcohol. In front of a mirror, vanity is in love with itself. Greed, the wealthy miser, is under the spell of money and possessions. There is a big difference in thoughts, emotions, and self-esteem amongst those who are wealthy and those who are poor. Wealth is not only the accumulation of material things, but may also refer to an abundance of anything, such as: *a wealth of creativity.* Multiple dimensions of various levels of the ego are constantly vibrating to trap us. We may think we are powerful because we have expensive and beautiful possessions, but the truth is, if we are not wealthy within, our state is one of poverty. All possessions stay in the material world when we die, but our Soul returns to its source of true wealth with all its kind and generous treasures of thought and deed.

The thief and the murderer are manifestations of mental states, of thoughts that vibrate at very low levels where false identity is mistaken for true Being. Spiritual reality is entirely overlooked. These mental states vibrate on levels of very inferior awareness. The multidimensional identities that we have created give us this connection to the world of illusion.

A Consciousness limited by fears, anger, resentment, and doubt will not make use of the elements necessary to wake up and maintain balance. States natural to Higher Being are created by our superior mind. Among them are health, prosperity, joy, Peace, compassion, philanthropy, and selfless service to others – all of which are expressions of Love.

Using our creative imagination, we can enter into the hidden places of the human mind.

Einstein said:*"In times of crisis, only imagination is more important than knowledge. It's during crises that great inventions, discoveries, and strategies are born."*

To overcome crises, we have to overcome ourselves. Crises represent challenges, the biggest one being to tame the ego. They offer opportunities to shine away our shadows.

When we confront our fears with realization, we discover how much energy they drain from us. We discover our true power, our inner strength. Our Light then vibrates more strongly and shines more brightly. Our true Being is the spark of Divinity within, fulfilling its dream of leaving the jail of ego. Little by little, the spiritual vibrations that we continually express begin to impact our Life.

Reflections

Unmask your ego and you will find the Light within you.

We get hooked by negative, conflictive news shows that nurture our need of these ego systems. Our culture is hardwired for negativity, and research tells us that the negative is a stronger influence than the positive. Studies show that people stare at "bad" images longer than at "good" ones, and remember bad experiences longer than good ones. Of 558 adjectives describing emotions in English, 62% represent negative ones.

The world of illusion holds us in its thrall. We feel so secure and protected within the confines of its darkness that we are afraid to leave it — we tremble if we separate from it.

The ego is continually calling the shots. If we so much as glimpse the Light, the ego will create confusion in us by stirring the pot and trying to envelop us again in its fog. We descend again and again, lost in its labyrinth of darkness.

Gandhi said: *"Without taking action, very little will be done. However, taking action can be hard and difficult. There can be much inner resistance."*

In order for things to change, we have to risk leaving our comfortable state and familiar fears, and have the faith to set out on a new road. We can fly to new heights and allow the currents of the wind to lift us up.

If you feel bad today, look and find someone who is in a worse situation than you — perhaps you can help them.

Overcoming any crisis enables us to improve ourselves.

Examine your negative words and your weak, dark thoughts and feelings. Constantly check to see if your actions are positive or negative.

Take responsibility for all of your thoughts, actions, words, emotions, and feelings.

Do they turn you into a victim?

If today you are suffering, you have the opportunity to turn that suffering around and open yourself up to hope and Light.

**Our thoughts, our actions, our words, our Peace are
all our own responsibility!**

When you feel that your thoughts bombard you, depress you, and hold you back, remember that they are *YOUR* thoughts, and nobody else's. The only person who can expose and conquer them is YOU.

We give our power away to our egos, and then we feel empty, disempowered.

When you feel confused, angry, or depressed, STOP! ... And *breathe ... Ask yourself if your thoughts arise from your ego, or if they are a whisper from your Soul.*

Just as the birds sing and fly every morning, I invite you to use your free will and your imagination. smile, sing, and fly.

Be the change and example for others.

Appreciate the opportunity to have multiple experiences in Life.

Discover your inner beauty, your power, and your freedom.

The outer force is the force of the ego, while the inner force is the force of the Light — our true inner strength.

My Notes:

_____

_____

_____

_____

The Colors of Life © 2000 Jacqueline Ripstein
Same painting seen under Normal & Black Lights.
Invisible Art and Light Technique © Pat

Lesson X

The Colors of Life©

" Clouds come floating into my life, no longer to carry rain or usher storm, but to add color to my sunset sky."
Rabindranath Tagore

Life with color is life; life without color is death.
Grey represents depression and numbness...Uncertainty.
The colors of life are synchronized with Faith. As long as there is Faith, there is Hope.
The Colors and the Light elevate us to vibrate with life.
Life is coded in one language—the Language of Light.
Light contains the sounds and colors that form a silent vibrational language.

Can you imagine life without color, seeing only in black and white? How would you feel? What would you be lacking?

Low-vibrational colors represent the loss of Joy and Hope.
Shades of gray confuse us; they hide the Light from us. We become depressed and our colors lose their glow.
The Heart does not judge; it keeps our Being in perfect balance. It doesn't know good or bad, only Love and Compassion.
Thought without feeling is like an arid landscape where nothing grows.
Emotion creates a feeling which in turn opens a portal to the Heart.

155

Our feelings are moved by prayer and gratitude. The Heart emanates our colors and connects them to the highest Heaven.

In this lesson we will discover how the Colors of Life move us, marking the rhythm of what we breathe, think, create, love, and live. They reflect how we feel. There are low- and high-vibrational dimensions of colors. The low drag us down; the higher vibrations of colors elevate us to the heavens, to the Light. As we focus on the Colors of Life, we balance emotion, thought, and Spirit.

To see life in black and white is to live in life's darkness, trapped in the miseries of our own captivity, where true Being remains inert as a result of a mind closed by illusion and depression. Joy is transformed into sadness, and this state molds our lives. All that we may see remains veiled because of a lack of Light. It is a state of blindness! White reveals the Light and black is the absence of Light.

We see and create our own reality. The colors relate directly to our emotions, influencing the mind and body, acting as much in the physical plane as in the mental and emotional.

Look again at this painting while letting the image speak to your heart. Do you want to focus your life on the lack of colors? Or do you prefer to focus on the Light and its colors that transmit a life of Joy, Love, and Peace?

During my exploration into the ultraviolet color vibrations to obtain what I called an *Invisible Technique,* it was my great surprise to discover that within this invisible world one finds octaves of colors that vibrate at different levels and that nourish and nurture our soul. I discovered that those colors have a special brilliance that differs from the range of the colors of the physical, material dimension. Within them are the most amazingly brilliant hues; they sparkle like the stars and galaxies in the universe and can be felt by their high vibrations. They flow and glow through harmonic codes and octaves. Even on my painter's palette these colors do not obey the laws of physics -- they contain a different configuration. They give a different result in their mixing, breaking all laws of material colors as we know them. Our Soul vibrates with these invisible colors that are picked up by humans, animals, and all of life.

I also realized that within the low vibrations of the infrared, the path becomes heavy and dark, igniting pain and darkness. This made me understand the great importance that colors play in our life and how they can reveal our awakening to life.

Our energy centers, or "chakras," are seven powerful systems of energetic vibration of color that connect us to life and the cosmos. They enable us to harmonize our body and flow with the rhythm of the universe. With our vibrations we create a silent language, a harmonious melody that awakens us and connects us to the beauty of life. They also mirror our mood and our hidden emotions. The color system must therefore be balanced for us to manifest a healthy, joyful, peaceful life.

Mother Nature rejoices in us, and through us as all life is interconnected. The ocean and its colors move our being; they move the water within us, the rivers that run through our veins, and the sun that illuminates us with its reds, oranges, and yellows, giving us a way to recharge our physical body and uplift our core energy. Just as the yellows connect us with our inner force, the oranges gives us the subtle energy of life, reinforcing our creativity and sensuality; the greens -- the vibration of the heart and the essence of life -- nourish and cure us, mediating between Heaven and Earth. The blues of the ocean and blues of the sky give to all beings the breath of life, which connects us to Heaven and awakens our desire to abide in the Spiritual World of our soul. We now come to the violets, the colors of the highest vibration. Violet connects, elevates, and awakens us to our Inner Being.

The colors of the physical world are always vibrating in harmony with Mother Nature, the universe, and us. When we see a sunrise, it inspires us. It's a silent language of nature welcoming a new day, an example we should follow. Just as the many colors of the invisible world reveal our inner energy (as seen in what we call the aura, whose emanations of Light can be shown using Kirlian photography) and the energy that gives life to all living matter, these invisible colors harmonize and connect us to the truth of life, to our Souls.

In a vibrant visible and invisible dance, the colors of life encourage us to breathe in divine inspirations. Colors such as white, violet, indigo, ultra-violet, and gold are our connection to the spiritual world and the highest vibrations of Peace and Consciousness.

When we focus on the present moment, our inner and outer vibrations of colors and the energetic system merge and become balanced. Living in the present moment is our only true reality—the future has not yet arrived, and the anchors of a past that no longer is, tie us down. Trapped in the illusory world, we enter the realm of egos, becoming slaves through our own will to vain hopes and fears that hinder us. The future has not yet occurred, but our thoughts and feelings of the present moment are creating this future life.

Living in the awareness of creating a positive and balanced life enables us to connect to a clear consciousness and to flow in cosmic harmony.

Life's colors are a clamorous signal to wake us up. Colors are the silent language of the Spirit and life itself. Animals express their essence through their colors. Life offers us multiple gifts through its colors—fruits and vegetables feed the body with their colors, and a feedback is created with our own energetic colors. Each color corresponds to a particular vibration and affects us in different ways. Every morning when we choose which color to wear, we connect unknowingly to the hidden, invisible language of our emotions. Each

The Colors of Life © 2000 Jacqueline Ripstein

Same painting seen under Black Light.
Invisible Art and Light Technique © Pat

day, life in the universe surrounding us sends the vibrations of color and sound that predominate in any given moment. If we pay attention, we will subtly perceive them and flow with the energy of life.

Let's analyze the color red, for example. This color has always been linked to Love. Through my art experience, and included in the hidden messages I have gotten, I've learned that energetically, every color has octaves and scales just as in music; both sounds and colors have lows and highs. The low scale of red represents the vibrations of anger, war, and manipulation; the high octave of red invites us to vibrate in love. The opposite of war...is love! In the same basic color we find the answer to how to create its opposite.

All situations of low intensity and darkness contain the seed of possibility to rise to a higher level; the colors reveal to us the secrets hidden within them. Isn't it incredible to see that the vibration of war inherently contains the potential to elevate to the opposite—to Love?

To see life through dark veils robs us of our true identity. We lose our freedom—it's like straining to see the sun on a cloudy day. If there are thick clouds blocking the sun from our sight, that doesn't mean the sun is not shining; it simply means that although it is hidden by an overlay of clouds, we are never lacking its Light. In like manner, the spirit, or energy, of our inner Light is confined within our body, and through awakening our consciousness we liberate it.

Our mission at birth in this dimension of life is to discover our Spirit, day by day.

Trapped in a false identity, our lives become gray and circumscribed. Ruled only by the material world, we fall off the precipice, and the veils of fear, anger, remorse, and depression fortify the illusion that envelops us. Not being true to who we really are, deception embraces us, masking our true essence, our authentic Being.

In the lower part of the painting we find one of the dimensions of darkness, a dimension where the material world blinds us, where we have been manipulated to accept our false identity. As we descend, the veils of denser gray increasingly block the entrance of the Light. The colors of life disappear and we see beings who, moved only by selfishness, are trapped in their own greed, lust, vanity, insatiability, and avarice. Such depraved beings -- wolves in sheep's clothing, searching tirelessly for vulnerable victims -- are shown in the lower part of the painting, together roaming with the ever-patient Death. Death enjoys seeing them asleep in a trance, already dead while seemingly still alive. This is their worst punishment.

The external force that entices us is weakness, while inner strength is our true force. Identifying, focusing on, and using the Light instead of darkness helps us to balance our lives.

To not give and share with others veils our Light. The colors of our system create energetic fields that connect us with all of life around us.

Most works of art emit vibrations that influence our energy field. Vibrations from art and music can have high or low frequencies, each connecting us to its corresponding emotions. This energy impacts us, distorting and depressing our engagement with life, or brightening and inspiring it.

A work of art that contains lower vibrations is connected to sad or listless feelings and emotions. Its corresponding colors and their sounds depress us and impact our energy system in a negative way. Although we don't see them, many things affect our magnetic field and energetic system. This is why we feel profoundly moved in the presence of art that is very inspirational.

The art we choose to have in our homes and the music we listen to are, at an unconscious level, manipulating our lives.

Some emanations of art, of colors, are so high and scintillating that they can create a bridge to other dimensions and levels of consciousness. But this also applies to low emanations. High frequencies of color that make our Spirit soar come from indigo, white, violet, gold, and ultraviolet; from these color vibrations, the body of Light emits the highest and most ethereal energy -- they connect us to the Divine Light. Yellow, red, orange, and green connect us to our material vibrations and our physical life.

The colors that constantly emanate from us attract people who are similar to us, those most in sync with the state of our own mental, spiritual, and emotional consciousness. *Like attracts like*, and those of similar vibrations attract each other, just as energy emanations also attract complementary situations. For example: A thought and emotion of depression will attract people or situations of that same level. An angry driver will "embrace" another angry driver in a collision.

It is essential to understand that the colors we emit are directly related to our thoughts and feelings. Without our knowing it, our colors connect to energetic portals.

Our brain reads and captures frequencies of sound and color -- usually an unconscious event. Many times we feel sped up, depressed, or angry, and we don't have any reason to feel like that, they are not even our own feelings, we could be sensing energies of anger and depression that travel through energy fields, we could also be perceiving this low emotions, and thought vibrations from human beings around us, their own low energy of thoughts and emotions can be very contagious. We human beings are extremely perceptive, we are not always aware of what our senses perceive, the only way to avoid picking up energies that are not ours, is to be aware of our own being.

The words that we speak are constantly creating sounds and colors that attract equivalent vibrations as they travel through different planes, seeking their resonance.

When we launch words that are low, rude, or hurtful in any way, they tie us to our egos and translate into a very low energy that vibrates in longitudes defined by certain colors. Red and black together generate power and control over us, including aggression, just as yellow creates joy, and violet connects us to our Soul.

When we enter a state of prayer and meditation, we are balancing our external being with our inner being, thereby realizing the one true reality. The Divinity hidden in our Being awakens us.

The energetic color of the heart—the color green—acts as our mediator, connecting us to balance and healing.

Any imbalance of our color system disconnects us from our Spiritual Heart.

If you feel off-balance, sick, or without energy, then you know something is seriously amiss and has to change. To turn your down feelings and thoughts into joyful ones, you could also start with being aware of our physical needs and health, knowing our body is "our temple". *How you are feeling connects you to the different energies of sadness, want, and failure, or those of Love and abundance.*

Your wishes and thoughts create what you receive.

Poverty is manifested in many different forms. Overall, it's a way of limiting ourselves to a small and constricted mind, deep within which is a profound sense of not being deserving of abundance, happiness, and health. Abundance is a state that includes plenitude, opulence, and every good thing.

A poverty mind is numb, asleep to the abundance that the Universe is eager to lavish on us. The gray colors of low self-esteem and depression choke off the flow of our capacity to receive. By accepting abundance we expand our consciousness.

Flashes of illumination come to us in moments of inspiration that let us see clearly our vastness. In the words of Giuseppe Ungaretti, *"m'illumino d'immenso"* "-- I illuminate myself with immensity". However, to ensure that this inspiration doesn't last, the system of the ego, aware of the threat to its existence, calls us rapidly back into a sleepy, dormant state. The world of illusion has its ways of ensnaring us -- drugs, alcohol, sex, and glamor -- that lull us into even deeper sleep. Stress, seeming lack of time, and problems that continually overwhelm us are tricks of the ego to keep us so busy that we forget about our Soul.

Leonardo da Vinci said that ***"Life is for living and death is for sleeping."***

Creation begins from Light, and it vibrates in multiple dimensions. The level of Light that we connect to will depend on the level of consciousness we achieve.

Birds begin singing at the exact moment when the Light begins to shine, announcing the awakening of life, which in turn inspires our own awakening.

Reflections

To focus on the Light is our choice. The different color hues represent different energies of life, including thoughts and emotions. Every color has a different vibration. The colors are our silent guides to discovering the invisible secrets of life.

All of our thoughts have a certain color. Our every action creates a color. Our words emanate colors. We are unique beings, and every person's identity is expressed through an energy system of colors and sounds. Each of us emanates a specific frequency – our "handle" -- that can pinpoint us individually better than any best friend, psychiatrist, or GPS. We are Beings of Light, vibrating colors and sounds through an invisible world.

By understanding how to use the colors of our energetic system, or chakras, we can affect our body and change our pattern of vibration. If we see that our energies are low, then aligning our color system and meditating in a shower of colors—white, gold, and violet—will elevate the vibration that is depressed and balance our system.

What color would you like to transmit?

Where the Light becomes brightest, the shadows converge into their darkest.

I invite you to listen every morning to the song of the birds encouraging you to receive the rays of Light that will illuminate your path every new day.

The lower octave of red underlies aggression and anger. The highest octave of the same color red immerses us in a state of Love.

Yellow elevates our joy, our life force and vitality.

And at the same time, a lack of connection to any of the inner colors of our system lowers our energy levels, creating an imbalance and lack of enjoyment in life. Many times, owing to negative feelings such as fears and pain, some of our chakra colors do not vibrate. If any of the seven colors are stopped, then our energy system is incomplete and out of balance.

Black debilitates us, absorbing our Light! It is the total absence of color.

When we awaken with gratitude, we vibrate with gratitude the whole day long.

The Light contains all colors, and the soul vibrates the colors of God invisibly. If our thoughts, words, and actions vibrate with Light, then we will know that our brief existence in this life has achieved its purpose.

Seeing the world as it really is and using our heart, instead of harsh judgment, is one of the principal lessons that we come to learn.

*E*very morning we awaken, lifting ourselves up to the Light of a new day! The colors of dawn vibrate in a dance of Love, as Nature wakes up…And what about us? Have we awakened from a long blur of being asleep, now aware of the Spirit within?

Every thought we think, every word we say, and every move we make vibrates a color. We emanate colors within our energy fields; this is our covenant with Mother Nature, with life, with God.

Connect to the Light daily! Let your vibrant silent language of colors guide you to the Divinity within you.

If, during the course of our lives, we awaken and rise above the darkness, if we escape from the prison of the ego, and through this freedom inspire the lives of others, then one by one we will bridge the road that unites Heaven and Earth.

Our body will be our vehicle, and our Spirit will be its guide.

Light, and everything contained within it, including vibrations of sound and color, is an encoded language that every cell and atom of our body understands.

My Notes:

_____

_____

_____

Life's Inferno © 2000 Jacqueline Ripstein

Lesson XI

Life's Inferno ©

"It is only when we have the courage to face things exactly as they are, without any self-deception or illusion, that a light will develop out of events by which the path to success may be recognized." I Ching

There is nothing worse than…Being dead while we are alive…

Being asleep while we are awake…

Letting the beauty of life pass us by, and seeing it through dark glasses.

When we are blind to the beauty of Life, we enter
Hell -- a situation of torment, confusion, or misery.

When we connect to darkness, we're not able to see the Light beyond.

We blame others for hurting us, but the pain we inflict on ourselves
sometimes goes beyond what others do to us.

The ego and its shadows create beliefs that cast us into life's inferno.

We often live internal wars even while peace reigns externally.

Hope, Faith, and your will to live will sustain you even when
your situation seems utterly hopeless.

The war inside us attracts and creates constant, discordant situations. Our internal war also creates illness in our bodies that replicate those feelings in a vicious circle (like cancer -- a physical, mental, and emotional mode of cellular aggression whereby the body attacks itself).

In this lesson we will look into the question of hell. Is it a dimension beyond life itself? Or is it a heavy-vibrational, obscure space wherein humans get imprisoned by their own lower, negative thoughts, feelings, words, and actions? Is it a place where, trapped by their shadows, the egos continuously veil their Light? Enter into an open space of conscious-awareness as you discover the light within darkness.

Overcoming and being aware of the ego, of darkness, is an essential aspect for us to realign, reaffirm, re-balance ourselves as we walk on the spiritual path. Our ego places a veil of illusion over us. It sustains and promotes our fears and our lower emotions. It distorts the way our mind perceives everything and mainly keeps us absorbed into darkness. As we fall into "hell" dimensions, the abyss generates a veil of amnesia that covers us, keeping us from accessing our higher wisdom and truth, our Light.

Hell in life indicates a state of suffering, of agony, of torture (by others, by circumstances, or by ourselves), and of insipid colors and little joy. Hell is a heavy vibration that drags us spiraling down from the highest to the lowest, darkest vibrations.

Hell can also be defined by every situation in which a person is forced to live in a painful, dangerous, or hostile environment. It can also be: an abusive relationship, a prolonged painful sickness, a combat zone, a personal loss, or a massive disaster.

Our thoughts can create hell. Negative thoughts are the most powerful magnets in the Universe. Once you have one negative thought, inevitably they begin to multiply, supporting the initial emotion that created it. They obscure our existence, overwhelm our minds, and blind us to every opportunity for experiencing joy and lucidity. We need constant awareness to monitor our thoughts and to change old, useless thought patterns; as they arise we need to extinguish them. This lesson's goal is to help you transcend the limitations of the ego, to help you focus your aims in the Light and not the darkness. As you recognize that you have the power to reach the Divine Kingdom, you raise your vibration and this increased awareness will guide you to identify the Divinity in yourself and in others.

The lower a human being descends, the more asleep and inhumane he becomes. Those beings that lack Compassion, Love, and Peace are the true targets of the ego system. Hell is a state of agony, torture, weakness, and blindness, of living in constant suffering, noise, anger, and hostility -- an internal and external war.

When we give our power to our weaknesses instead of to our strengths, we fall into the first circle of darkness.

We suffer, either immediately or later, for all our negative actions, because every action leaves an active, energetic footprint vibrating behind us. If it is low, we create dark, heavy energy, popularly referred to as "bad karma." And we will carry these energies with us until the day we leave our physical body, taking them along as part of our energy debt-- -- unless we "clean up our acts" before we die.

To be in a "living hell" is to be a slave, imprisoned by our own egos. The world of illusion traps us.

We have the potential to elevate ourselves to a heavenly existence or to fall into the deepest of hells.

In Dante's *Divine Comedy*, we read the inscription on the gates to hell, which applies just as much to modern man as to those in Dante's day:

"Through me is the way to the city of woe; through me is the way to eternal pain; through me is the way among the people lost; justice moved my sublime architect; I was constructed by divine omnipotence, supreme wisdom, and primordial love. Before me nothing had been created except the eternal, and eternally I abide. Abandon all hope, ye who enter here." Dante Alighieri (1) The Divine Comedy.

How does someone fall into hell?

Have you heard these ideas, or expressed any of them in a moment of anger? Are they uttered casually, by chance, or do they reveal actual situations and levels of human hell?

They say if we are bad we will go to hell...

If you commit a mortal sin, you will go directly to hell...

Hell is a place of eternal torment of the condemned...

Sinners go to hell (some in a hand-basket)...

When there is pain and discord anywhere, we regard these experiences as a "living hell"...

(1) DANTE, ALIGHIERI (1265–1321). Italian. Writer, poet, literary theorist, moral philosopher, and political thinker. Born in Florence, writer of the great work, The Divine Comedy. Considered to be one of the most significant figures of universal literature. Admired for his spirituality and profound intellect.

Bad language, harsh judgment, and rumors about others bring us to a state of darkness...

Have you had a hellish experience?

Have you lived through war and the hellish pain that it generates?

I am already in hell!

What a hellish life I am living!

Go to hell and leave me alone! (Or for the prim and proper: Go to H-E-double toothpicks!)

Little by little, primitive, lower consciousness and energy may descend upon the person until very little conscious awareness remains. The tortured human then spirals through the many lower dimensions. In one such state, the person may become satisfied just to survive -- among them are the masses that live the "unexamined life," despaired of by Socrates. A person may, of course, descend further: a deeper sleep state numbs many through addiction to alcohol, drugs, and sex. Many find perverse amusement and release in hurting others, mercilessly striking out with their fists, guns, or tongue, and lacking all empathy and compassion. Dazzled and bewildered, nurtured by the lowest emotions and by the lowest "pleasures" of material life, they descend to the inferno levels of inhuman existence, habitually creating and attracting more and more negativity into their lives and the lives of others. This is a lifeless existence in which excitement, drama, cruelty, and aggression are mistaken for the true purpose of a human life.

The primary source of all existence is to "BE" the Divine link.
Material strength and power alone, absent inner strength, is weakness.
Inner harmony and strength are true power.

Faith crumbles along the way, love all but vanishes, and the law of fairness is forgotten – but what is generated will come back more forcefully, keeping the law of karma in constant motion.

"I am lost! I am confused! Everything has become dark! Who am I? Where Am I? Why don't I see the LIGHT?"

As we lose our way, we give our power to others, people who complement our ego system perfectly. Becoming numb as the lower forces take over, we start moving farther and farther away from the heart. We lose our balance and degrade ourselves; we stray from the road of Light and the path becomes ever darker. Now that lower instincts have been awakened, ego is joyful and stimulated. It will now obscure, bit by bit, the Light of its victim.

If we see a glass as being half empty because it contains little water, without seeing that the "empty" space in the same glass is full of particles of Light, this short view limits our life experiences.

Every time I create a painting, a process of alchemy happens. I become one with it; thus guided, I merge inside of the images as if by pure magic. If I paint a fish, I become the fish; if I paint a horse, I feel the essence of this beautiful animal throughout my entire being. If I paint joy, my heart's portal opens wide. When I paint heaven, my being rejoices in the Light. I feel sparkles all over me as Love, hope, and compassion awaken me.

If I paint pain, sorrow fills my being. When I started this painting, I was living a hellish situation, as I had fallen into a setting with wolves in sheep's clothing, attracting them through my fears and insecurities. The past awakens as sadness, mourning, rejection, and aggression. Moments of heartbreak are pulled from the deepest recesses of my memory as I remember the many hurts I have endured. Tears roll down my face as I feel the pain of not only my own life, but that of other human beings!

With each brushstroke of this lesson's painting, I entered a human inferno. While painting, I felt and heard the anguished voices of pain, furor, and terror emerging from the sub-human levels that were revealed to me. Caught inside a descending spiral, I did not like the sensations I was experiencing. I knew that I had descended because I was feeling more and more pain, uneasiness, and heaviness. This spiral descended in narrowing concentric circles, their vibrations ever lower and more restricting.

This work of art showed me that it is impossible to ascend from the lowest and heaviest low-vibrational circles without passing through certain tribulations and difficult life tests. Depending upon what level he is rising from, the tormented person rises up only by his own efforts to awaken. After confronting the many shadows that he has attracted and fed within himself, a challenging process has to evolve: the hidden-ego beings of the lower dimensions must be exposed and defeated. Such "beings," which do take on a kind of "life" of their own, are often devoid of all empathy, coupled with such ruthless cruelty that they defy the very concept of "human" beings.

Depression is one version of hell on earth. It unleashes despair, hopelessness, pain, and sadness. When we help ourselves, we take a step towards our healing.

Depression and anxieties are associated with the gray colors. Different shades of gray can depict: lack of color, lack of confidence, and lack of energy, as well as dampness and depression. Pure gray is the only color that has no direct psychological properties.

Weighted down by our own negative thoughts, words, and actions, we begin our descent into the so-called "hellish" realms. It is the descent into this slow-moving spiral, a spiral that actually turns counterclockwise – in direct opposition to the clockwise spin of the chakras -- that drags us down toward vibrations that emanate from the "dirty red" colors. Moving slower and slower, our descent penetrates the black realms of non-light existence and spirals toward infra-red frequencies.

Infra is defined as "underneath."

We lose our humanity when we fall into the infra-human. We become not only inhuman, but also inhumane.

Infra-human behavior and thoughts spawn low frequencies that are incompatible with heavenly realms, resulting in the hellish environments that we create "down" here. The loss of Faith, Hope, and the Charity born of empathy diminishes our potential to raise ourselves up.

This painting depicts the different hells: torture -- a realm of evil and suffering, of deceit, of falseness, of darkness; the hell that we ourselves can make of our lives, the hell into which we may fall from the weight of our egoic actions. Heavy, coarse, and vibrating densely, these actions retard our growth. If we don't seek to cleanse and refine our vibrations, our soul will fall and remain anchored. Even when liberated from the body, it will be surrounded by beings that have also created a hell, a place from which one cannot free oneself so easily.

Every civilization has spoken to us about the existence of some form of good and evil, heaven and hell.

The ancient Egyptians, for example, had elaborate beliefs about death and the afterlife. Perhaps the most famous and important chapter in The Egyptian Book of the Dead is titled, "The Judgment of the Dead." In court-like proceedings, the deceased presents that which weighs most heavily on his heart (involving conscience and morality) before the counsel of Osiris. By overcoming a test, he may continue on his way in the world of the dead, the Duat, until he reaches the eternally fertile fields of Aaru. This chapter (number 125), well known for its complexity and length, contains the so-called "negative confessions"-- declarations of innocence that the deceased made in the presence of the gods of the court, after justifying his personal actions. This chapter was clearly of great moral significance to the ancient Egyptians.

At Osiris's court, *the Spirit of the deceased was guided by the god Anubis. Anubis magically drew out the Ib (the petitioner's heart, representing his conscience and morality) and deposited it on one side of the scale. The heart was counterbalanced on the other side by the feather of Maat (Goddess of Truth and Universal Justice).*

Meanwhile, a court composed of gods formulated questions about the deceased's earthly conduct, and depending on the responses, the heart became lighter or heavier. With Osiris assuming the mantle of ruler of the dead, the role of Anubis became that of guardian to the departed soul. At the conclusion of the court, Osiris handed down the sentence.

The ancient Egyptians believed that a human soul was made up of five parts: the Ib (heart); the Sheut (shadow); the Ren (name); the Ba (soul); and the Ka (vital spark). These parts would go to meet the mummy and form the Aj (the beneficial being) that would enjoy eternal life in Aaru (paradise).

We can't escape. One way or another, sooner or later, we will suffer the consequences of all our actions.

One of the hardest realities for some of us is to accept that our actions have consequences. Whatever we do either affects others or us. We may fool ourselves, but the darkness and weight of the energy leaves an impression in our Soul. ***The law of Karma has been activated.***

Although it is natural for humans to long for paradise, there exist many situations beyond our control, which can create a living hell such as accidents, war, and natural catastrophes. It is how the victims react to these situations that determines the kind of hell in which they will find themselves.

What kinds of people cast themselves into hells?

They are dense, negative people whose actions and thoughts have a very low and slow, heavy vibration. Often they have caused extreme harm to others, whether physically or emotionally, by their ugly thoughts and deeds. Using their loose tongues as knives, they attempt to hurt the soul of their victim. Inevitably, one day this energy will be confronted by Divine Justice and will have to face its related energy consequences.

Anytime you judge someone, you reveal more about your own weaknesses. Do not judge—or you too will be judged.

The worst of the hells is the torture of our own mind! *Tortured by our own thoughts, we remain subjected to this penance for as long as the mind harbors falsehood.*

Without realizing it, we fall from one level to the next, bouncing around chaotically. *Anger and fear trap us and run us down.* We lose trust in ourselves and then in others. Stumbling, we fall from one hell into another.

The word inhumane may be ascribed to people who, dwelling in lower levels of consciousness, lack compassion and are cruel to an almost unbelievable degree.

By stunning contrast, the humane person is operating from the highest vibrational levels, truly manifesting the Light of our Creator in his or her actions toward others. The humane person is kind, humble, compassionate, understanding, considerate, loving, lenient, merciful, forgiving, generous, benevolent, and charitable – a truly humane, human being.

In this painting I used darkness, grays, to show separation between the light and colors of being in heaven and the darkness of being in hell. Dark, greyish colors symbolize confusion, a lack of light, I always use dark colors to emphasize and reveal the Light. Mixing various colors creates dark tones, and each color absorbs certain frequencies of Light. Thus, on the palette of life, as negative emotions arise, we diminish our Light.

Our own shadows, our egos, offer the clue to revealing our Light.

Colors both represent and produce emotions.

Black is the absence of Light. Darkness is perceived as absence of Light. When you focus on the fiery colors in the painting, you will feel how black debilitates us; the red connected to the lower octave evokes revenge and anger. Lower emotions emanate lower color frequencies; they absorb our Light and depress our energetic system. As we lose our balance, faith, and hope, our colors fade and lose all shine. When people fall into infernal levels, their light is not only veiled, but is also absorbed by darkness.

Why do we fear the darkness? We become fragile because our low-vibrational feelings are devoid of Light. Darkness is the abode of depression, fear, jealousy, uncertainty, confusion, and a host of other destabilizing emotions.

Take five minutes to meditate while looking at this painting. Whisper to your inner being: *"Please, God, remind me of my light essence. Show me daily who I really AM."*

When we evaluate our experiences, we see that none are bad or good -- they are simply life experiences. There are moments of happiness just as there are moments of sadness and joy, smiles and tears, rising and falling, successes and failures. We shape our paradise, or hell, or limbo according to how we treat our fellow man and ourselves. *Cause and Effect is a law... What we sow, we really do reap.*

The planes of consciousness are wide-ranging; one may take an awareness journey from the lowest vibrations to the highest, from hell to heaven.

To justify our own discordant actions as the result of the power of others over us does not absolve us of responsibility; neither does it diminish the karmic vibratory energy that will come back to us.

Forgiveness – of self and others -- removes this cord, this chain, and sets our karma free; no longer are we drawn to or tied to those who still sleep. Forgiveness elevates us to the Light.

Forgive those who have caused you harm and accept that you cannot change them. Forgiving them and seeing them with compassion presents love in its greatest glory. You will be free of the burden of resentment. Forgive yourself in order to move on and to lighten your load. Leave all burden, guilt, pain, and anger behind.

In painful situations, try to connect to stillness. Your will to live and to "beat the odds" will sustain you even when your situation seems utterly hopeless.

Keep calm! Your attitude is your ally. Realistically assess your situation. Gather your resources. Force yourself to connect to positive thoughts; negative thinking will only proliferate and overwhelm your mind.

Always try to remain calm and think! Fear and panic obscure our intuition and our clear discerning.

Take a few breaths to compose yourself. If you let fear overrule common sense and critical thinking, then you set yourself up for a series of mistakes.

One attains compassion when one has lived through painful experiences. Having suffered certain experiences ourselves, we can then understand the suffering of other beings.

When I finished the painting of hell, the sorrow and heaviness in my heart was huge. My connection to levels of fear, pain, and aggression was too strong. I saw that I had not been able to escape.... I had to leave these infernal vibrations the moment I realized where I was being taken. Suddenly the image of an Angel appeared in my mind. I followed it and it showed me that this same painting could spark Hope and Faith in all who writhe and burn in the fires of torture, of hell; it would help them see that there is salvation.

My wish is that the messages within this painting serve as a beacon of Hope, promoting the belief of positive outcomes in events and circumstances in your life; to help you gain the Hope of always knowing that Heaven is open to all who are willing to step in, to forgive, to forget, to let go of all anger and resentment and to awaken to the truth. We are Divine Light Beings living a physical experience.

Reflections

The triumph of good over evil has been an intrinsic part of the journey of human beings. Countless histories show us that in the end, good wins over all the tribulations occasioned by evil. Focus your heart and thoughts on acting with goodness, Love, and compassion. Light dispels the shadows.

We project to the world through our emotions, thoughts, and feelings.

When referring to cruel conditions, treatment, behavior, etc., *inhuman* is the lowest vibrational level to which a human may descend.

To be inhumane means "to have become...unkind, cruel, showing lack of compassion towards other alive beings."

Forgiveness doesn't just go for each other but back to us too.

We can learn from the ancient Egyptians. Their advanced studies and knowledge of human nature, along with their ideas about the afterlife, give us much to ponder. They understood that at the end of life, we take with us all of the actions and human experiences that we have had, and that our ultimate goal is for our heart--which is made up of our every experience -- to become light, until it is as light as a feather.

Even before the words come out, our minds have already assumed and accepted the thoughts and feelings behind them, that what we are about to say is true. Be very careful with your words, as once you have hurled them, there is no calling them back! They can hurt as easily as they can create, and their energetic legacy continues.

First is the thought, and then comes the word and the talk.
What we say affects our lives: our thoughts do the programming
and the words manifest the reality, our reality.

When you talk about your problems, your focus is on the problems, not on the solution. The negative thoughts can grow stronger and stronger, and then they can overwhelm us.

Judgment and negative expectation are ways of creating resistance; their hard energy hurts us before they hurt anyone else.

To embrace our fears and our shadows, to forgive and love, we must let go of all lower emotions and focus on the Light. This is how we step out of *Life's inferno*.

Our lack of self-respect and feelings of unworthiness put us in a state of vulnerability. This may take the form of helping and attending to the needs of others while forgetting about our own. Then we become hurt and angry. Reverse it! See your worth and give yourself time, love, and attention. If you don't do so and continue to feel unworthy, others will see you that way as well. They will simply not notice that you too wish to be respected, cared for, and loved.

Sometimes, unaware, we perpetuate our role as victims. This shows our lack of self-love.

Throughout our lives, most of us repress, or at least suppress, our unhappy feelings. This festering load of what's popularly referred to as "stuff" -- anger, jealousy, blame, and resentment -- makes our cargo heavier. To lighten this burden, we must leave behind all that weighs us down. For good reason, when we are in a state of pain we say, "My heart aches."

Pain of the heart can even attract illnesses related to that state, for whenever love -- the energy of this organ and all bodily systems -- is obstructed, illness will manifest.

The actions that serve to lighten our being are: forgiveness, compassion, letting go, humility, Love, and awareness that we are children of the Creator, carrying within us the Divine Spark. We are Light!

When people say negative things, take heed! That energy is a disease that is very contagious. Don't participate in it! Leave it alone and close your mind to all negativity by focusing on positive words and ideas.

The voice of conscience cannot be stilled and will follow us everywhere. We betray ourselves when we lie and don't honor our word, and when we lack integrity in any situation.

Our fear of death has many faces. Carrying a load of painful feelings -- while leaving behind loved ones, attainments, and possessions that we know we can't take with us -- coupled with fear of the death process itself, makes for a most unappealing prospect! Worse, believing that we are finite and not infinite and eternal can take much of the joy out of living!

Our ability to correct negative thoughts and actions enables us to reach an elevated state.

Heaven is open to all who are willing to see beyond their egos.

Why wait for death in order to be free?

It is now, in this precise moment as you are reading these words, that the magic begins. Once we set foot upon the road and receive the inspiration that nourishes our soul, the journey to Divinity begins...The door opens. Will you enter?

Heaven and hell are alternate dimensions separated by vibrational frequencies that our ordinary senses cannot detect. We create our life's experiences from the particular level of our consciousness and energy, and thus we create our own heaven and hell.

*I*magine... You're climbing a steep mountain, and your mind is filling up with heavy, low-vibrational thoughts of past pains and present burdens. Your energetic body becomes heavy, slow. It makes ascension difficult.

Remember that one negative thought amplifies itself continuously.

Forgive yourself in order to forgive others.
Honor and respect yourself. In Faith and simple willingness, be liberated from the heavy loads you could be carrying.
Forgiving and letting go enable your ascent to higher consciousness and facilitate your enlightenment.
By discarding all that is fearful and false, you will rise!
And your heart will be lighter than a feather.

Although there are clouds in the sky, the sun is always illuminating everything. Look beyond the dark clouds and you will find the Light.

Stop in front of a mirror and, in sacred silence, Love the Being that you see.

Color vibrations realign, reaffirm, and re-balance us.
Never quit! Don't lose Hope!
In order to have any chance at all of surviving, don't let go of Faith.
Know that All will be OK!

My Notes:

_____
_____
_____
_____

Masquerade © 1996 Jacqueline Ripstein

Lesson XII

Masquerade©

"The world is a theater curtain behind which they hide the deepest secrets."
Rabindranath Tagore

Life is a grand stage where humans appear.

Seconds and minutes pass, turning into years.

Civilizations leave their footprints.

Every action we make leaves an energetic print.

We are actors and actresses in the great theater of life itself.

Tragedy and comedy are opposites, and we are here to experience it all.

We are eternal students because knowledge is so vast.

Teachers continue being students.

We are the directors, producers, and actors in the stage of our life.

The wardrobe changes, but the performance and feelings of the
human being remain the same.

Life is a tragedy for those who prolong suffering.

And comedy for those who smile and rise above trials and dare
to be brilliant.

Stop repeating painful life lessons: learn the lesson and move on...

We are here to discover the reality of love...

Love needs no mask.

$\mathcal{L}$et the show begin -- the tragedy, the comedy, the melodrama... All are episodes in the Great Theater of Life.

This lesson will help you identify more clearly our illusory world and the ego's many identities. It will help us expose our masks, discovering that behind all masks we often find fear and confusion. Without their shield we expose the real us. There is a very fine line that separates laughter and sorrow, comedy and tragedy, pain and suffering. To discover that line is part of our task. We mask ourselves as a means of protection – to conceal our fear of rejection and other painful feelings. Many times we wear smiley-faced masks when everything in our lives is crashing down around us. The masks camouflage our fears of vulnerability, of failure, of shame, of low self-esteem. These masks give the illusion of self-confidence, so that even when we really feel worthless, we become part of a masquerade, tricking ourselves as we pull people's attention away from our true selves.

To reveal our true self we need to remove all masks and false identities. It takes courage to admit that we are weak and fragile, or that we feel lonely. To understand how to face our weaknesses, fears, and struggles is an essential step we need to take on the path to discovering what our heart and soul are crying for. This painting can help you identify the masquerade, as you learn to be comfortable in your own skin, as you start loving and accepting yourself. Nobody is perfect; we all have our own struggles. The learning process never stops. The Angel of Death at the right-hand side of the painting comes to raise us up, showing us that death is only physical; our Soul is Eternal.

"All the world's a stage, and all the men and women merely players; they have their exits and their entrances..." William Shakespeare.

At any given time, life can be a comedy, a drama, a tragedy, or an exhilarating adventure. Life offers us diverse experiences, many of which we create ourselves, while others seem to pop up on their own along our path. From the time of our birth we begin to adapt, learning from the environment and everyone around us. Little by little we learn to take care of ourselves, protecting ourselves from pain. We seek ways of best dealing with our problems, ways that end up becoming habits of our personality. If not seen through, false identities isolate and disable us. Afraid that others will judge us or laugh at us, we hide under masks, also known as personas (the Latin word for theatrical masks).

When we use masks, we can't even perceive that we are hiding our true feelings. Not allowing ourselves – let alone others! – To see our vulnerability feeds inner weakness, because rather than confronting our true self, we hide it.

What lies behind the masks?

The human being is born naked, without masks.

This "nakedness" also represents purity -- the innocence we are born with. There is a veil that covers most of us; as we grow older, this veil obscures direct connection to the Spiritual Dimension.

Masks hide what we think and feel. Masks conceal our fears, our fear of judgment, creates resistance. Fears hide within fears. Behind these fears lies the fear of rejection, of loneliness, of abandonment. We cover up to protect ourselves, and we use masks to shelter our true Inner Being. Masks are created in the world of illusion from unhappy and fearful thoughts and feelings. They can make our faces ugly and our lives miserable.

Spirit needs no cover-ups, no masks.

Disguises are shaped by the uncertainty of not knowing who we truly are and from fearing that others will see us as a failure. We may worry that they can peek into the low self-esteem we feel. We may try to cover up what we believe are our flaws and failings; feeling incomplete, we fiercely protect our false identities. We insulate our true feelings with impenetrable layers that offer the illusion of protection. And the more layers we add, the more we block our experience of Love and Life.

The mask of tragedy covers the agony, distress, and fears that lie within us. It conceals our low self-esteem and low-vibrational feelings, depicting intense suffering.

The mask of comedy assumes a false appearance of perpetual cheerfulness to cover the pain we are suffering. To fit in with our society, and be accepted, we "play the game" – along with most other people. Joy needs no disguises.

True happiness needs no mask. It nurtures our hope and faith. A smile keeps us healthy and revitalizes us. Taking life less seriously, we find joy rising up above all trials of life. When we quiet our minds, we become more aware.

Do these masks provide the true personhood that we seek? Or does stripping off the masks and finding ourselves "naked" enable us to glimpse the truth of who we truly are?

The masks serve to cover up our fears and feelings of worthlessness. They help us to conceal our trembling and inconsistent ego, with the aim of hiding our assumed fragility. Right along, beneath the mask, is the possibility of embracing who we really are, discovering our love and living our truth. Unmasked, our essence, which is beautiful, and our true identity, which is fearless, are freed.

> *"For years, copying other people, I tried to know myself.*
> *From within, I couldn't decide what to do.*
> *Unable to see, I heard my name being called.*
> *Then I walked outside." Rumi*

Masquerade© 1996 Jacqueline Ripstein

Same painting seen under Black Light.
Invisible Art and Light Technique © Pat

Masquerade © 1996 Jacqueline Ripstein

Same painting seen under Normal & Black Lights.
Invisible Art and Light Technique © Pat

Looking at ourselves in the mirror, what do we see? Do we see the image reflected from the mask, or do we see the human being of Light that shines through our eyes?

If we don't like our life the way it is, then we are the only ones responsible for making any needed changes.

This painting expresses the human experience that for centuries has played a leading role in the theater of life: it is here that identities are sustained by the ego system. The painting Masquerade reminds us that the physical body is mortal but the Spirit that gives it Life is eternal.

We see the masks at the foot of the stairs...broken. The steps represent centuries of masquerades. How long have we worn masks? Is it not time to rid ourselves of them and create a new reality? Without them, we are free to be and embrace our Light.

The beggar situated on the left side of the painting throws money. He represents humanity that has wandered for eons in search of its true dwelling place, the forgotten and veiled home within. Here, material things are of little significance.

To the right is the queen, transparent as an illusion: she is a human being.

Every human being is important on life's stage. If this were not so, then why would life have so many players?

Illusion traps us in its web and confuses us with the idea that it is reality, and that we are at its mercy.

The invisible world reveals the truth.

Sometimes we use our masks in a rather jocular and burlesque kind of way, celebrating or mocking them as we attempt to describe ourselves through them. But behind all the joshing, one finds the truth. We know that these masks cannot honestly express joy or pain, and we see how clearly we hide them both.

As we participate in this dizzying masquerade, we become more and more confused! When we allow the material world to give us a false identity, we ascribe our true worth to it. How can anyone be *"worth more"* by driving an expensive car or adorning their wrist with a gold watch? When we focus on values in the material world, we not only lose awareness of our own true value , we lose contact with the reality of our Spirit.

We sell ourselves so cheap!

When a piggy bank makes a rattling sound, it's because it is empty inside. When someone brags about how much they have, they are simply showing us that they are not connected to their real value; their inner reality has become as a stranger.

Little by little, generation after generation, we have become more and more materialistic and our essential worth has gotten lost in the shuffle.

Are we not tired of twirling on the ballroom floor in a seemingly endless masquerade?

I invite you to meditate on this painting and look honestly at your reality. Look at where you have placed your worth, your time, your Love.

We are living in times of social, financial, and environmental chaos, but perhaps these events have a purpose. Could that purpose be to shake us to the core, revealing to us that we have been living a lie -- and that money and status can offer but a temporary salve? Money is energy, an exchange of energies for goods and services. Unfortunately, much of our money has been stained with the blood of low-vibrational actions. Its once-simple purpose for trade has become corrupted as our attachment to material things intensifies. Love of mammon has become so great that it might even be considered a kind of "second fall."

Speeding against time is consuming our lives; stress is killing us. Feeling that time is in short supply and "running out" on us, we chase after it. Not enough time! Trapped in this system of fears, we strive to live moments of quality.

Time in Life is precious -- a gift, not a burden. Our moments of joy nourish us. Peace is tonic to our system; in and outside of time, Love is the essence of our Soul.

Trying to live attached to an identity that is represented by masks takes us farther away from our true essence. Too often we try to fill this existential void with food, vacation homes, jewelry, and other material goods. But when we are devoid of Love, none of those objects can replace true Love. We are left to confront reality and see the trap that we ourselves have set. Our civilization has come to a dead end. Now is the time of our wake-up call, a time to strip ourselves of lower emotions and move closer to our truth, to Love. When we learn to love ourselves, we rise up and enrich our lives and the lives of others.

Our children are stressed and confused. Infected with ways of "playing" that involve violent fantasies, some are starting to kill each other! This is a symptom of a critically ill society. We want to give our children all we can, so we teach them the values that we ourselves have learned. We try to give them our best love, but we are also teaching them to cover themselves up and to seek what others have. Little by little they lose contact with their true essence. We are educating them to be inauthentic, to wear masks and take on identities. They basically learn that they are bodies and not Spirits on a physical journey. Imagine how our world would change if we could totally overhaul our educational systems! Teaching children from early ages the concept of unity, not separation, while encouraging them to be who they truly are, would constitute the fourth "R" – readin', 'ritin', 'rithmetic, and reality. But educators, no matter how enlightened they may be, are not in a position to reveal what a child's mission in life should be. Children must be allowed and encouraged to discover it for themselves.

In the material world, money feels temporarily fulfilling, but in our spiritual reality money means nothing, nor can it buy love. The collapse of this *material illusion* will create *much suffering* for us *if our self-esteem and identity depend on it.* Our inner strength will carry us through all the storms; it will help us rise up after we fall.

Love is our ultimate source of abundance.

Without Love the material plane is empty. Nothing can really satisfy us, fill us up. Absent love, our search is eternal.

In ancient times, masks were used to represent myths and human emotions. Greek actors, for instance, wore masks to represent the muses of tragedy and comedy, Melpomene (crying) and Thalia (laughing). This way the audience – especially those seated at a distance -- could better recognize the actors' emotions and identify their own.

In this painting we see the two angels -- the Angel of Life, who is delivering us into this life, and at the other pole, the Angel of Death, who is receiving us when we "die".

Between the Angel of Life and the Angel of Death is a determined space and time that is our brief visit to life; this time span is different for every being. Many souls return to the Spirit world very soon after birth -- these great beings' mission is to enter this dimension to help bring about change in their parents' and other caretakers' consciousness and circumstances. Our main goal in Life is to re-encounter Spirit and learn to manifest an enlightened life. Human experiences and Love give us true wealth.

You can also see in the painting that the masks are broken. Masks blind us. Identities cover our truth. They disguise our true Self and conceal our Light. When we gather the strength to rip off these masks and dare to be ourselves, our life flows freely with no limitations. We can then connect to our true essence in the Invisible World, cradle of the Spirit. Everything then changes as true destiny manifests.

We also see on the left that the Book of Life under the Angel of Life is open; the journey begins -- the opportunity to live, learn, grow, and shine has been ignited. On the other side, one finds the Book of Death closed, and that the queen has disappeared; the material game is over and the true Light journey has begun. Life on this plane is over. The Angel is transporting the Soul back to its core.

Behind the masks, we are living stories. They can be happy stories or trouble-laden stories; most are incomplete stories, marked by our brief and narrow perception of life. When we are able to discard all masks, then our true identity arises, our perception expands and our Spirit shines through all life experiences.

Ask yourself: What is Life? What is death? What did I come here to learn? What is my true mission? The Angel of Death patiently awaits our time to depart and will be calling on us at any moment. He returns us to our original home, guiding us through the Invisible World while protecting us with Light and showing us our true identity. He shows us our authentic truth that there is no death, and that all that has happened to us had a higher purpose all along. The body goes back to its birthplace, and the Soul returns back to its source as well.

If the Angel of Death waits for us, then consider the question: *Is there no death?* What do you think? Write about it in your notes from this lesson.

Reflections

This painting invites us to think things over, to reflect on our life's journey. May it help us to identify our false identities, to clearly see the Light, and to shine away all darkness. Is life an illusion? A Masquerade? Life seen through the ego and only through the veils of the material reality deceives our true purpose, how we perceive life is what creates the illusion.

Life is a journey to wake up from the dream to the awakened state.

Life stories are merely...stories. They belong to the past.

In moments of silence, discover your masks; see the reasons why you use them. Write about it in this lesson, and once you can identify the masks, you can discard them. Like magical art, they will disappear.

Vices trap us when we feel undeserving of Joy, Love, and Light and render us numb and impervious to these nurturing qualities.

Our so-called *defects* show us that we don't come here to be perfect. Perfection does not exist at the level of human life. Wanting to be perfect is an egoistic illusion: to stand out and be "a cut above the rest," one cultivates an image that is elevated and winsome. If we were perfect we would not be in this dimension of life; we are here to learn and emanate more LIGHT!

Live every moment of your life with passion; give your best smile and your kindest words and deeds. You are the one creating your life, a life that touches every other life.

Don't complain about or dread your tomorrow. Instead, give thanks that you are likely to be alive to enjoy it.

When we say "yes" but really want to say "no," we are living a lie dictated by the ego and portrayed by a perpetually grinning mask.

When we are not true to what we think and feel, we fall victim to the veil, and what we veil is the truth of our identity. We escape from our truth and the masquerade begins.

Our fear of solitude and rejection makes us disguise ourselves more and more, sometimes to the point of imitating others. Fear of the unknown is one of the reasons why we do not make the effort to change. Venture off and create a new path—one that is full of new adventures where joy, love, and abundance flow readily to you.

The only death is that of the physical body, and with it go the illusions that have made us believe that we are this physical matter. A "living death" is the worst death that we can face. Ultimately, one's spiritual qualities and talents will reveal their inner Being. And at that moment all masks will disintegrate. Rather than a mere sheep, the awakened one will now become qualified to lead his life.

With every word we speak, we create, and it manifests in our senses and energy vibration. Think twice before speaking; listen -- listen very deeply -- to the thoughts and the words as they are arising in your head. Let the Spirit of Grace and Truth refine the words before they leave your mouth.

Our very guarded fear of failure, born of the ideal self-image we have created, both terrifies and debilitates us, taking us farther away from our essence.

Are you ready to re-create yourself? Do you dare to be you? *To love yourself and to shine your Light?*

Silence offers a great opportunity to listen to your heart's desires.

If you are not able to remedy a problem that confronts you, stop and breathe...and reprise this lesson. Everything seems bigger from close up, where we give it more importance. If you back up and gaze from a distance, as you would before a work of art, you will see your challenge in a different light; the "picture" will seem smaller, and you will not blow features that are nearest to you out of proportion. You will see with different eyes and you will find new solutions.

By dropping the masks that conceal our pain,
we expose our vulnerability, our fears, and our suffering,
and give ourselves the opportunity to heal our wounds.

Dare to be yourself! Strip yourself of your fears!

Dare to take risks and make changes that will take you to
unknown territories, opening doors along the way that
were previously locked to you.

All human beings have needs. The most important of these
are to be appreciated and loved.

Take off the disguise. You are unique. Find your strength.
Remember that every word, every action,
and every thought we have marks us with a permanent,
energetic soul-print.

Life is a journey to enjoy, not a race against time.

Do not fear death! Fear living your life asleep, dead, and
ignorant of your human and Divine rights. Death liberates us
and takes us to Eternal Life. Don't fear so-called "death"
anymore. Look at the Angel who will receive you. By "dying"
we simply return to our essence of LIGHT.

Ego is illusion and dream.
Spirit is reality.

Love needs no covering, no mask,
and no disguise.

Immortality lies within each human being.

My Notes:

_____
_____
_____
_____

Eternal Love © 1997 Jacqueline Ripstein

Lesson XIII

Eternal Love©

Love transforms poverty into riches, the pauper into the prince."
Rumi

A second.
A caress.
A thought.
A Feeling of Love!
Eternal Love is unconditional.
It is immortal.
When Love is based solely in the physical plane
Its true essence is lost.
LOVE IS to recognize our Inner Being, our Spirit.
LOVE IS to love myself first so I can fully love you.
LOVE IS to feel with the heart.
LOVE IS a journey, where we discover new, higher levels of Love.
LOVE IS to understand the flaws and appreciate the virtues of others.
LOVE IS to do service for others.
LOVE IS to live with joy and gratitude.
LOVE IS to forgive.
LOVE IS to learn to give, and learn to receive.
LOVE IS the connection to our Spirit.
LOVE IS the activation within us of Compassion.
LOVE IS to know God.
LOVE IS...the Bridge to Eternity.

Give thanks to Life. Smile at this opportunity to experience more Love.

This painting reveals to us that Love is the Supreme Lesson of life; without love a human existence is empty. The mastery of life is to find that love within ourselves, and then share it with all humans, animals, and all life upon planet Earth. Love has many levels. As we expand our love of self, our capacity to love others grows. As we love others, our capability to Love expands. As we practice service and Compassion, we connect to the deeper vibrations of pure unconditional Love. Love is the highest emotion and the highest state. As we learn how lack of Love brings to us insecurity, fears, and an unhealthy and unbalanced state of being, we can then shift our lives to a balanced, harmonic, peaceful existence. Love is the reflection of God within each of us.

Immature love says: 'I love you because I need you.' Mature love says: 'I need you because I love you.' Erich Fromm

What is the purpose of painful experiences? The answer is to comprehensively teach, inspire, and empower us toward self-realization as spiritual beings so that we can shine our Light.

The energy of Love is Life itself.

Love is a topic that evokes in us humans more interest and passion than any other. Some consider it our biggest enigma. Sometimes I ask myself if in this lifetime we will be able to realize the purest, most unconditional and eternal vibrations of pure Love.

Love has many facets that correspond to very high vibrations. In order to access these vibrations, we need to control our emotions and see through hostility, anger, fear, envy, depression, and all the other negative expressions of ego. Many times we are so busy in our lives, we are unaware of our indifference toward others' needs.

Eternal Love © 1997 Jacqueline Ripstein
Same painting seen under Normal & Black Lights.
Invisible Art and Light Technique © Pat

***We are loved to the same degree that we love, neither more nor less.
Egos obscure the power of Love.***

We are multidimensional beings, and our Love expresses in many ways. We Love our parents, children, partner, animals...To Love life itself is our supreme existential experience. Love surrounds us in every way; we are awash in a Sea of Love. But all these different expressions are simply sparks of the same Light. True Love is manifested within us. It is the essence of our Creator. Loving ourselves, we go within and accept ourselves as we are, forgiving ourselves for our mistakes. We do the best we can in the moment we have acted. If our consciousness were higher, we would have been able to act differently. When we discover Love within ourselves, we begin to vibrate with life, with Mother Earth and her children. *Unconditional love is the ultimate lesson as we learn to love others and ourselves, without any fears or expectation...generously, and in an unlimited way.*

We are not observers in our lives; we are co-creating it every second.

The most sublime manifestations of Love are compassion and service.

Compassion happens when we are able to sympathize with others people's feelings and pain, and have in our hearts a strong desire to alleviate their suffering.

Love is a non-ending source to heal others and ourselves.

Love goes hand in hand with the development of different states of consciousness, which determine our spiritual levels.

The different states of Consciousness range from a zero level of awareness, meaning to be asleep in life and lacking the ability to perceive, to feel, or to be conscious of events/self/others/the environment. As we "awaken," we acquire higher levels of self-awareness; we start accepting responsibility for our actions and our lives. Too often, painful experiences stop us from wanting to move forward, but as we forgive, clear away anger and resentment, and learn to love ourselves, we then rise to higher vibrational levels of "Being." We move forward as we become more aware of and responsible for our fears, our thoughts, and our actions. Love evolves into Compassion and helps us rise to the highest Universal Cosmic Consciousness.

Gratitude is the key to Love.

The lowest level comes when we lack Love within ourselves; it is then that we leave empty an energetic space that is filled with lower feelings, which we vainly mistake for Love. We are the receptors and transmitters of thoughts and feelings; these energies create realities! We need to take full responsibility for what we are creating.

The Love we give reflects the unlimited potential of the Love we bear within us.

Take a minute and look at the painting of this lesson, Eternal Love. You can see that the bodies are merging into the sky. While painting it, I could constantly hear this whisper:

We live in a world of illusion.

We love a man, or we love a woman, but we also contain both within ourselves; female and male are within us, showing us that there is no separation. We are all One.

We try to own the person whom we Love.

We are afraid of losing him or her.

But we cannot lose what cannot be lost.

Nor can we lose what does not belong to us.

Unconditional Love gives Light to a moment of inspiration, a magical moment that makes our inner Being, our Spirit, vibrate.

Love is Eternal.

If we neglect to water a rose, it dies. Similarly, Love for a person or a thing requires constant nourishment. We all require attention and love. Without them our lives would be empty and dry...like the dying rose... and we would lose all sense of joyfulness.

Love never hides; it's waiting for us to discover it.

Lack of Love causes us to live in pain, anguish, and loneliness. We desperately seek someone to Love in order to feel complete, protected, and loved.

Are we in Love with people? Or with our own need for Love? Life without love is ultimately life without meaning.

When Love within us is weak, we ourselves are weakened. We lose Light and inner strength. Our will becomes compromised. We fall prisoner to the ego system. As a result of this weakness, we lack the insight that accompanies Love. We look everywhere to receive fragments of love, and we tend to follow those who make false promises in the name of Love.

**The fear of losing a relationship leads us, inevitably,
to the loss of that relationship.**

Meditate on this phrase: "To fall down on the ground is not the problem; to fall in love with the stone is!"

When our lives are filled with love, we become empowered. When they are full of fears we become disempowered.

There are different ways we love: love among family members and between friends; an avid desire or enjoyment of an activity; romantic and passion shared by two lovers. In all its forms, love is... Love.

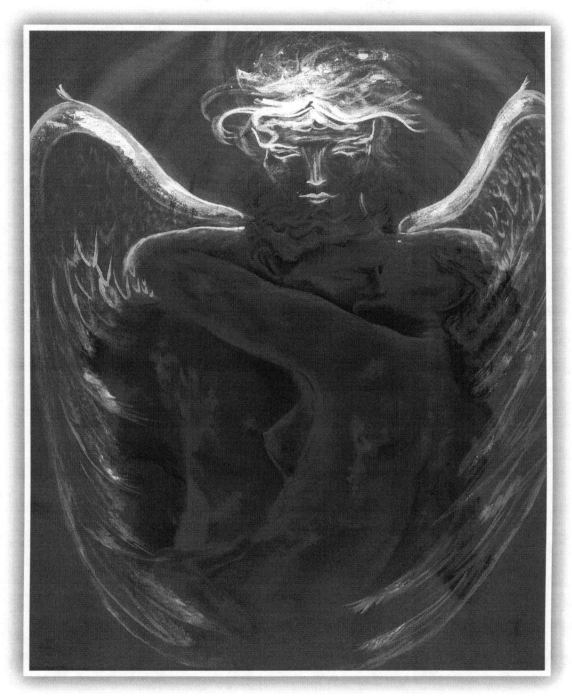

Eternal Love© 1997 Jacqueline Ripstein

Same painting seen under Black Light.
Invisible Art and Light Technique © Pat

The difference between love and unconditional love lies in the origins of their purpose and the emotional energy involved in each. If in our aim to love someone we experience such feelings as: dependency, control, loneliness, anger, fear, low self-esteem, our own selfish needs...then we know that our love is limited, is lacking in strength, and cannot satisfy us. It becomes an incomplete ritual, one that can come to an end at any moment. This love is deficient; it's temporary.

Unconditional Love is unlimited, boundless, and infinite. It is truly without end because its vibrations are eternal. As we learn to love beyond any judgment and without fears, we become aware of our powers, of our light. Love then expands us. True Love never perishes. It is everlasting.

Fears reproduce and multiply into more fears.

Fears feed other fears, ensnaring us in their many webs. The result is confusion, mistrust, and separation. As we loosen the reins of our lives, we hand control of our will to others.

Fear is a shadow; Love is pure Light.

It has been scientifically demonstrated that the energy of a person near us affects our own energy, and vice versa. Fears and low vibrations are highly contagious. One has to be very aware in order to not become infected by them. We live in a civilization that harbors more fears than ever before. We are bombarded with negative news that reinforce fear.

Loving ourselves fortifies and enlightens our lives.

We have suffered enough, collectively and individually. We have acquired a tendency to cling to both suffering and the identity of sufferer. By not taking responsibility of our actions, we fall into the role of victims. By not letting go of the past and its painful experiences, we anchor our growth and our wakefulness. Most people regard pain as a natural life experience.

Pain is inevitable. Suffering is dragging that pain along and using it as a crutch; it nurtures the ego system and veils our Light.

Constant suffering and pain can awaken us, for they give us hints that suffering ends when we learn from our life lessons, such as the necessity to Love ourselves.

Suffering reveals to us that we are lacking Love.

We are living through key moments of an Awakening Humanity. We have the choice to recover Faith, Hope, Love, and Compassion, both individually and as Humanity.

Love nourishes our life.

If we lack self-love, we cannot fully love others.

Pure Love is born of the union of two souls.

Love has the vibratory force needed to connect us from the Earth to Heaven.

True Love feeds Faith and Hope, since they are both born of Love.

Loves gives us the valor and the necessary strength to overcome any adversity.

Love "loves" miracles into being. It gives us the will and the power to rise up to heaven. All roses have thorns. Every action has a consequent reaction. Our task is to learn to balance our lives. Among the opposites of Love are: indifference, fear, hate, egoism, and aggression. Nevertheless, the idea that there is only one short step from Love to hate is very real, and many people have experienced this phenomenon to some extent.

Dr. David R. Hawkins (1) tells us that failure, suffering, and illness are the result of the influence of patterns of low attractions; and that success, happiness, and health come from the patterns of powerful attractions or energy.

Lifting ourselves up today to new vibratory fields is essential in order to be an active element of an Era of Change. Let's move with awareness away from everything negative that weighs us down and causes harm; it is the first step we need to take in elevating our vibrational field.

Difficult moments require that we know how to confront and dismantle our fears. To do this, we must rise above the fears to a level higher than the one from which they were created.

To gain life mastery and to be able to create the life we truly want, it is essential that we constantly be aware of our feelings. Feelings are the "automatic pilot" behind the driver and are responsible for every outcome. We could repeat a positive affirmation on a daily basis, but if we feel depressed, the order to create abundance is filtered through a depressing lower rate of vibration, attracting the opposite of what we've affirmed.

It's the emotion that hides behind the thoughts and words that promotes the energy attraction.

The presence or absence of Love is what determines the outcome of our feelings and of our whole life's journey. It underscores our strengths and our weaknesses. The lesson begins as we learn to Love ourselves, and then in how we express our Love for others.

If I see love, I have that love within me. If I see beauty, I am part of that vision. If I see hatred, that hatred is inside of me. If I see evil in you, it is only that same wickedness in me that allows me to recognize it in you. So beware: whatever trait you recognize in someone else, be sure to look for it first in you.

I perceive in you what I refuse to see in myself.

As we learn to refine and control our thoughts, words, and the actions they generate, we become the captain of our life. Be careful about what you think and say; invite positive forces to guide your life. Try to spend time with or listen to people whose vibrational field is higher than yours. Surround yourself with positive thoughts and feelings. Listen to inspiring music. And above all, try to Love unconditionally. This simple willingness and these efforts will raise your vibrational field.

> ***Love goes beyond our physical death; it's embedded for eternity in our Souls...it is Eternal Love.***

You will begin to awaken to a life full of happiness, Love, respect, and inspiration.

It is Love that motivates us to live!

Love Life and the opportunity we have to be in it.

Love the day and the night.

Love the wind and the fire!

Love Life! Love death!

Love, Love, Love.

Raising ourselves up to the vibratory dimensions of Love and Compassion will give us the life of Peace that so many of us yearn for. Fears crumble when we transcend the level of Non-Love. ***Fears crumble like broken seashells battered by the waves when we transcend...***

As we become more understanding and caring, opportunities will present themselves to us with greater clarity than before.

Dr. David R. Hawkins (1) was an internationally renowned psychiatrist, physician, researcher, and pioneer in the fields of consciousness and spirituality. Utilizing techniques derived from kinesiology, he presented a method for measuring truth (or consciousness) on a scale of 1 to 1000, where 1 is simply being alive and 1000 is the highest attainable level for a physical human. In his book, Power vs. Force, Dr. David R. Hawkins presents a hierarchy of levels of human consciousness. From the bottom to the top, the levels of consciousness are: shame, guilt, apathy, grief, fear, desire, anger, and pride, followed by the positive levels of courage, neutrality, willingness, acceptance, reason, Love, joy, peace, and enlightenment.

"Love is misunderstood to be an emotion; actually, it's a state of awareness, a way of being in the world, a way of seeing oneself and others. It's being considerate of others. That's all, just considerate, patient, and kind. Being content and able to enjoy life in all its expressions is more important than anything as you get older." Dr. David R. Hawkins (1)

It sometimes feels as if there is a single step between Love and hate; we experience this when the level of Love is so low it seems to slide to its opposite side, where fear, anger, resentment, and hurt reign. When the intensity and intimacy of love turns sour, hate may be generated. These inferior feelings transport us to the lowest vibrational fields, where Love is absent.

When "Love" "easily slides" into fear, that means it wasn't "Love."

If you find yourself in a difficult moment when you are being confronted by hostility, and the defenses that exacerbate your fears are activated, TRY TO REMOVE YOURSELF FROM THE SITUATION FOR A MINUTE...AND BREATHE!

1. Dr. David R. Hawkins was an internationally renowned psychiatrist, physician, researcher, and pioneer in the fields of consciousness and spirituality. Utilizing techniques derived from kinesiology, he presented a method for measuring truth (or consciousness) on a scale of 1 to 1000, where 1 is simply being alive and 1000 is the highest attainable level for a physical human.

Physically take a step back, look for water and wet your face. By creating distance --you will feel a moment of alertness, a spark of Light.

You will consciously create a physical and mental distance between yourself, the situation, and the lower emotions. Water is the actuality and symbol of "putting out the fire." This distance will give you space for a moment of awareness. As time passes by, we have the opportunity to overcome painful experiences; it helps in our healing process. Time heals all wounds, but it's what you do to heal the wounds while time passes that determines the speed and efficacy of the healing process.

Our sorrows and wounds can be healed only when we reopen them and confront them by using forgiveness as our tool and love as our guide. Then we can let those loads go and recover our joy for living.

If the aggression was such that you were offended, humiliated, abused, or physically hurt, then the task is to try to understand what you can learn from it. Why was this experience attracted into your life? Was it a wake-up call?

Nothing happens to us by chance; all we encounter has a purpose. What aspect within you needs to be strengthened?

Learning to forgive others is a process that frees us from our own venom, venom that bonds with hatred, pain, and fear. As we forgive, we ascend in consciousness. Forgiveness does not have to mean being close to those who cause us pain; if they are unrepentant, forgive them in your heart and distance yourself from them. Distance heals.

To not forgive others is to be tied to them by an invisible cord that energetically binds us to them until we cut it. And the only way we can cut this cord is by learning to let go, by forgiving. The result is inner peace. Love and harmony will then fill our being.

Reflections

To Love all human beings in the present moment is to know that within them sparkles the same light that shines within you.

Learning to Love is the ultimate test that determines the mastery of our lives.

To awaken to life is to take responsibility for our lives and actions. To learn self-love is a key to moving on to a power that is greater than ourselves, a power that helps us to move forward and guides us into higher levels of awareness.

To be conscious of empathy and compassion enlightens our life.

We may turn our attention to being Lovers, Lovers of Eternal Love.

Two feelings shape our lives: Love and fear. Fear is the most limiting emotion: it weighs us down with anxieties about losing what we believe belongs to us. Love creates Peace, harmony, and balance. Love is our Divine State, our conduit to our Creator.

Negative emotions such as attachment, jealousy, and blame arise from the lack of Love; they lower us to lesser levels of vibration and generate feelings that are opposed to Love, such as rage, indifference, and hatred.

The low vibrations attract us with great force. They can be very "exciting." When they awaken our lower self, we inevitably start attracting lower vibrational events and people.

Lower thoughts and words create lower actions.

The ego keeps us far away from pure Love; the ego and Love are incompatible.

Angels and Divine beings rejoice in feeling us vibrate with Love.

Love is state of bliss that elevates us to the highest levels of vibration and transports us to the sacred realms of Life.

The lack of Love drags us down.

The seed of Love is planted inside every human being.

The Forces of Light protect us when we Love.

Love is an Invisible vibratory force that elevates, illuminates, and connects us to our Spirit.

You decide which road to take. There are no roses without thorns, and all our decisions have a consequence.

If you are willing to pay the price of your actions, then go ahead and be responsible for all their reactions and consequences.

Ascension is realized after we strip ourselves of what weighs us down, including all fears. We can then leave in the past all that doesn't belong to our present moment.

Being "lightweight" is a prerequisite to living "Lighter." We have less weight. As we become "brighter," we then begin to vibrate much faster; this vibration transports us to the higher levels of consciousness wherein Love abides.

To live in the vibration of Love makes our lives blossom!
We then can shine our Light onto others.

Remember that every action has a consequence, and we must accept and learn from it.

Egos achieve; Souls realize.

Only when we learn to Love ourselves can we Love others.

Unconditional Love is the Supreme Lesson of Life.

Behind every negative emotion one finds fear. And behind every positive emotion one finds LOVE.

As we lighten and light up...we become enlightened.
Dare to Love, and your Being will
vibrate with Light and Joy.
Life is the journey;
Love is the Destination.

My Notes:

_____

_____

_____

_____

The Garden of the Prophets © 1982 Jacqueline Ripstein

Lesson XIV

The Garden of the Prophets©

As above, so below; as below, so above....
The Principle of Correspondence states that there is a harmony, agreement,
and correspondence between these planes, delineated as:
The Great Physical Plane, The Great Mental Plane, and The Great Spiritual
Plane...The Kybalion.

A glimpse of Heaven...

Knowledge enables Man to reason intelligently from the Known to the Unknown.

Within a human being a whole Universe is manifested.

The Principle of Correspondence portrays the Truth between the laws and
energy phenomena of the various planes of Being and Life.

Life's journey is full of varied experiences.
Sometimes we are "up" and sometimes we feel "down."

The Heartbeat of Life... Happens as we flow and beat to the rhythm of life and Love.

We all experience sorrows, joys, hopes, pain, love...All of these states are helpful
in bringing us back to our true essence, our Spirit.

Every life experience, without exception, points us to the profound
inner mystery that will reveal our Light.

The essence of Light is Infinite and never- ending.
In silence, Spirit reigns over the World.

The Prophet is an intermediary between humanity and Divinity.
All human beings can be prophets if they can perceive
God's Light in their hearts.

ears are created by the ego system to hold us back, to stop us from being brilliant and from discovering our Light, our truth. They make life murky by veiling our light. All infinite and never-ending things are beyond the limitations of the mind, and the essence of Life itself is infinite.

This painting's lesson is a guide to help us reveal our magnificence; it shows us how our role in life can affect the whole universal system. Each living being is an essential link in life's expression, and we each have a unique purpose for our existence. We are meant to be brilliant, to dwell in glory! This painting reveals a powerful key, how we also hold within us the power to destroy. The time has come for each of us to awaken, to realize our responsibilities and learn to honor all living kingdoms. We must stop the barbaric killing and torture not only of humans, but of animals as well. Animals are not trophies or commodities to serve our pride and greed; they are part of life's magnificence, and they have their own energetic purposes.

As awareness increasingly awakens within us, we can heal ourselves and help heal Mother Earth while we become beacons of Light in a World of Love and Peace. This painting evokes our heart center; its mission is to be a source of inspiration. It inspires us to live life with gratitude as we awaken and live in a state of holiness.

INSPIRE...take a breath...and see this painting again. Let its energy uplift you and unite you with your higher self.

We are all spiritual beings living a human experience unfolding on the same planet. We are *One human family,* each of us going through his or her own apprenticeship. Not only are we individuals living in particular societies of which we are integral parts; we are at the same time parts of the same civilization. If we destroy our planet, we destroy our home; by taking good care of it and all life upon it, we are leaving a home for our children where they may evolve and experience a peaceful, loving life.

Our role is that of guardians, not of destroyers.

This painting, *Garden of the Prophets,* created in 1982, turned out to be a great revelation. My art has always been my teacher and my guide. Each painting reveals to me hidden messages encoded within the invisibility of life. The paintings have helped me to transmute into higher levels of creativity and inspiration. For me, *Art is the language of the Soul, a silent language that speaks from one heart to another heart. It connects us to the most subtle aspects of consciousness. During moments of great inspiration, its vision helps us unite to all of life, inspiring in us Hope.*

Art is born mysteriously. Artists are guided by a mystical force powerful enough to impel them to create. Wherever the state of mind and consciousness of the artist may be, that is the level from which he or she will creatively express. High inspirational artwork is born of a spark of the Soul; it vibrates, and contains within it the essence of cosmic life. Its mission is to influence the observers and transport them to higher emotional and spiritual states. If the work of art is created from low emotional vibrations, without much input from the Soul, then the effect on the observer -- even if one is not aware of it -- is direct transmission of those low-energy vibrations, with attendant feelings of sadness or gloom.

A work of art that tries to imitate the beauty of creation by reproducing it on a flat canvas will inevitably fail, as its resources are very limited. The artist has limited physical resources with which to create a work of art, but when imagination is added, and the Soul is the creator of that art, then life is imparted onto a canvas. The artwork then takes on a life of its own and vibrates at higher levels of consciousness.

Works of art are born from creative forces arising spontaneously within the artist. Creativity and imagination free the individual from limitations of both the body and mind.

In a work of art that is alive, its atoms vibrate and the image emanates high-vibrational energy to the observer. Combined, the vibrations of colors, symbols, and images result in a truly *living* work of art that influences all its surroundings.

When the body dances, the Soul rejoices!

When through our Soul we sing, the Divine Being is heard.

Art reveals to me secrets embedded within invisible dimensions; each painting teaches me concealed knowlege about life. Following certain rituals that I perform before painting, within seconds, a state of meditation flows throughout my being, transporting me to those remote realms where all of life is conceived and created. Hours may pass, but in reality they are instants; when we connect to the Soul dimensions, time does not exist. I'm just the brush, the instrument that brings in the messages, and when I "come back," I myself can barely believe I made that piece of art. At the same time, it gives me great joy to be able to inspire the lives of other human beings. For this reason, I feel a great responsibility to share what the Creator has shared with me.

This painting in particular helped me to understand the vision of a vaster world -- the union of everything. Is it a prophecy or a warning to our humanity? It helped me understand how small we are in the face of creation, and yet, at the same time, it helped me appreciate the individual impact we all have on the cosmos. We must recognize that today we are not living in ordinary and predictable times. Clearly, the world we thought we knew has changed, and no longer can we live in lower states of consciousness. Those who do will inevitably start "short- circuiting" with the higher frequencies that are coming in. That is, all thoughts and actions resulting from low consciousness will bring an instant "payback," one even stronger than the force that created them. This payback can manifest in various ways, from poor health to being on the receiving end of misdeeds similar to our own.

Those who are aware that we need to pursue a path of Light to benefit humanity will be rewarded for -- and by -- their every good deed.

Our every thought, word, and action influences the destiny of the rest of humanity -- from our children and their progeny into the unending future. We must be alert to reverse as much as we can the damage we have done to our planet. Our every action reverberates not only in other human beings, but also in the ecosystems that Mother Earth continuously sustains, and is therefore a part of the universe.

Goodness is itself its own reward.

Even if we adopt neutrality, the lack of positive connection will manifest an energy that is negative for us. In not offering our positive force, our energy is applied, by default, to all negative vibrations.

This is for me the main message to receive through this painting. The Prophets invite us to observe the destiny of our humanity from a higher place. What do we choose? Continue living in war? Why not finally be the creators of world peace? The decision is entirely in our own hands.

We see the Earth in the center of the picture.

Our planet Earth is a living entity with myriad manifestations of life. It is our schoolhouse, where we go to learn and discover who we truly are. It is our opportunity for deepening and refinement as we enter into Divine Consciousness.

This painting sounds the clarion call to wake up from a prolonged sleep.

It is a time of great caring and respect.

Mother Earth is a living entity who moves within an intelligent universe. Everything that exists has a certain vibration -- from a stone to a plant to an animal to a human being. The difference between the vibrations of the different kingdoms, from mineral to human, lies in the speed at which vibrations move their molecules.

A stone in the mineral kingdom pulsates very slowly, but within that kingdom there are variations; crystals and precious and semi-precious stones have higher levels of vibration: the green kingdom presents increasingly higher vibrations, while those of animals are higher still. All kingdoms vibrate at different frequencies, and the highest subtle vibrations may be reached by human beings. Among human beings there is obviously a wide range of vibrations, from the lowest to very high levels of awareness. As beings who are both human and divine, it is our responsibility to restore, sustain, nurture, honor, and respect all living beings upon our planet.

We know that Gaia, the Earth, is a living entity that harbors all of life. It follows a universal flow of evolutionary and energetic vibrations in which the surrounding universe also vibrates, and it develops and changes according to its own parameters of energy and evolutionary cycles. This vibratory phenomenon affects human and all other forms of life on Earth.

The Earth has its own pulsation and vibration, which is adversely affected by the low vibrations of suspicion, selfishness, hatred, and war -- negativity that acts like a cancer in our planet's energy system, just as it does in the human body.

Every cell has its own life. If the cell stops vibrating with light, it becomes debilitated and is attacked by carcinogenic agents (darkness and blackness denote lack of Light). Slowly that "darkness within us" invades the body, gradually absorbing its Light, its life, its vital energy. The body is left in darkness — the light goes out and death arrives. On planet Earth, every individual is an interdependent cell. If our behavior is negative -- coming from a low vibration -- we will pass these negative vibrations, this negativity, along to others, diminishing their possibility of living a life of Light, Love, and Peace.

We are all pure energy that vibrates at a certain frequency, with each frequency emitting a particular color and sound; this emanation expresses our emotional energetic level. Measuring it would help reveal the level of consciousness that we have in that moment and the next level to strive for. The emanation of sounds and colors changes continously, according to our emotions, thoughts, and actions. These color emanations and the sounds they silently emit are registered and felt by all human beings and animals.

Through the centuries, prophets, mystics, seers, and beings who have reached high states of Consciousness have revealed humanity's destiny through words -- philosophies and texts that were written with keen awareness of Cosmic Connections.

As you observe the painting again, I invite you to use your imagination and feel the inner Being that is part of your eternal existence. Take a deep breath in this instant. Remind yourself that you are a Divine Soul and let the Light illuminate and guide you. Let your Being manifest truth and inner beauty. Discover your mission in life.

I now will share with you my own experience while doing this work... Before I start painting, I reverently dedicate my brush to God. As I prepare my palette and materials, the canvas invites me to enter higher states of consciousness. When my eyes start flickering, I know this is the signal that I'm being raised to higher states of inspiration. The *paintbrush then connects to the Cosmic Solar Light,* depicting the clouds of Heaven.

The wind blows gently. The blue and violet colors represent inspiration; they represent the spiritual realms. The beauty of the heavenly sky activates our divine qualities.

The Light that illuminates everything constitutes an inexhaustible source of joy that brightens our eyes as it feeds our Spirit. In the lower part of the painting, we see a blend of reds and oranges, announcing the dawn of a new day. It is the dawn that invites humanity to awaken and to take an inner journey. This art emanates vibrations that connect to our heart and inspires us to reconnect with our Divinity. Every Prophet leads us by the hand to the crossroads where the ego, through the world of illusion, has trapped us in order to keep us in its labyrinth of darkness.

I invite you to connect with each Prophet and, within the silence of your heart, listen to the messages that the Cosmic Light can reveal to you.

"Look at Planet Earth and world events, and you can clearly see powerful changes happening. They can become increasingly destructive, or we can turn around and use the crises as an opportunity to evolve and ascend."

The first Prophet in the painting calls to us, inviting us to evaluate the situation...Peace, unity, time, and aggression, Are we as One Humanity ready to overcome all of our fears, and move into a space of higher consciousness and Peace? Listen within the sacred silence of our hearts...

The choice is ours.

Allow your imagination to lead you on this mystical journey with the purpose of realizing awareness and healing. *Ask yourself, What role do I play within the Life of the Planet?* Immerse yourself in purposeful contemplation and reflection. Feel peace, love, and light. *Inhale, and enter these higher dimensions to discover your truth and awaken to your humanity.* We have unlimited discoveries ahead, the most important of which is the unleashing of our extraordinary creative potential, and with it the awakening of Divinity within each of us.

The second Prophet in the painting tells us: "How much time remains to lose or regain world peace? Peace is a gift that you have not accepted; it is the natural state of your Soul."

"Is Peace leaving you? Humanity has constantly been faced with the disasters of war, malice, greed, and negativity -- a monotonously dysfunctional cycle." We need to code a new program, to create a new holistic approach to all of life on the planet, whereby we inform all our actions with Compassion. Only then will our children receive the benefits of a new harmonic humanity. Negative vibrations are as well symptoms of an internal war, an indication that we are connecting only to our physical existence, sustained by the many shadows of the ego system. This false connection creates in us anguish, bitterness, pain, uneasiness, and great dissatisfaction. It creates stress and deprives us of inner peace. There is a void -- the connection to our Soul is missing. Internal war generates external war. To achieve World Peace, we must, one by one, find inner peace by connecting to our true Source of Being. We are a Divine Soul; the body is just the carrier of that particular Sparkle of Divine Light. It is essential that we not participate in mental or physical acts of war. Even when we are vehemently opposed to war, we are fanning its negative flames. Rather, we need to be... PRO-PEACE. Whatever we focus our attention on, we increase the energy of; we pass hostility on to our children, perpetuating a harmful environment. Nobody wins in war if there are injuries or deaths.

As we learn to balance our energetic system, we discover our inner peace and connection to *Universal Love.* We recognize that in the universe, there is no separation; all is One. When we are unbalanced, we feel lonely and neglected -- as if we are empty -- and try to fill up that emptiness in a thousand ways. This lack of Supreme Love underlies the notion of separation.

Through meditation, or a moment of inspiration, we can discover
our Divinity, and by connecting with our Divine Light,
realize the state of inner peace.

The third Prophet emphasizes *time*: *"How much time do we still have?"*
Life and time move around a material plane. If we leave the planet without
our bodies, the notion and usefulness of linear "time" cease to exist in the
familiar sense. Ask yourself: What is time, and how does it influence me?
What am I doing with my life while seconds constantly pass on this earthly
plane? Is it a second, a season, or an eternity in which I exist? Is Life a
space or an interval for the Soul to learn more? Or is it part of eternity
itself? Is it a cycle? Life gives us the opportunity to learn, to grow, to wake
up. *Life passes in the blink of an eye —*

The body is limited by time; the Soul is liberated from it.

We call the space between every second the Present. A line is composed
of a sequence of points, but we see only the line and not the points. In the
same way, the present is the only reality, even when the mind transports us
to the past and the future. Present time is not the product of the mind. It is
the mind that focuses on the "present" time—if you decide to do that. If we
are present, we participate in our lives; to not be in the present moment is to
live in the absence of our lives. Every instant of time in the present creates an
event. The present is a gift that we receive if we live in the present.

The past is the result of life experiences and emotions etched in the mind,
but they no longer exist in the present moment. Only through these thoughts
do we constantly reconnect to past events, buying into the illusion that they
are still present. The future is the product of the imagination -- it has yet to
be created. It is the energy of the emotions and thoughts that we have today
that will create our future experiences.

The first point of entrance into the rigid, physical dimension of time is birth, and the exit is, of course, at physical death.

Physical death liberates the Soul back to its Light Source.

The fourth Prophet represents *Faith and Hope*. In meditation, see within yourself, and visualize the awakening and ascent of a New Humanity.

Faith helps us hold on to life. It shelters us in moments of turbulence. It nourishes in us Hope and strengthens our sense of certainty, confidence, and conviction. If we lose Faith, we fall into the clutches of the ego, with all its skepticism and doubt. Insecurity invades us.

Hope keeps us alive, active, and empowered.

"Break the habit of aggression," says the ***fifth Prophet***. "Lay down your weapons! The evidence that humanity has fallen to very low levels of cruelty can be seen by children killing or torturing helpless creatures, and even other children."

Aggression attracts aggression.

When we attack other human beings we violate their very beingness; abusively, we impose our will to gain control. We forget that all attacks will eventually backfire.

Peace nurtures Peace.

The antidote to aggression lies in peacefulness as we learn to know ourselves, finding within us the space for Inner Peace, for doing service for others, giving help, protection, and cooperation. All these actions elevate our consciousness, reminding us of our essential unity. Compassion born of love is our highest expression.

At the entrance to the Higher Heaven, we see the Archangel with the Book of Life. Our next step takes us to a review of our lives, including all of our days, our words, and our actions...Archangel Michael welcomes you. "Will you be inscribed in the Book of Life?" Take your time to think about all he is saying to you. "Have you learned your life's lessons? Were you able to wake up to your life? Did you love and respect yourself and others, and always maintain your integrity? Follow your journey, dear one! Welcome new challenges as opportunities, and use the Light of your Being to guide you on your way."

Each Angel has its own vibration. The Archangels are the highest ones, as they are closest to our Creator. Archangel Michael protects and guides us through the darkness and helps us realize our life's purpose.

An atom is an atom, whether it is part of the earth – of vegetation, of animals – or of a human being. All material forms, as well as higher beings, are defined by different gradations on an energetic scale; they are fundamentally alive by the same energy and they all *vibrate*. Their differences stem from their levels of vibration. All are creations of the Light, and they exist within the infinite mind of Oneness. *All things* were created with and as love!

What does the change we are living through stem from?

As I mentioned previously, all people create their own reality depending on their thoughts, words, and actions. These define their frequency of vibration. Each "reality" is therefore valid for the person who created it, for it corresponds to its own level of vibration. It is also expressed by a unique corresponding emanation of color and sound. Every human being is unique. If we had a video camera that captured only the emanations of color and sound from humans and other life-forms, as well as the vibration of the planet, it would give us a symphony of music and a spectacle of unique colors that we have never before experienced.

Fears intercept our signals! They disrupt our connection to the Light.

Whenever we assert that another individual is wrong in feeling a certain way, it shows our inability to view other people's experiences from their own reality. This reality is the result of the experiences that person has had and learned from.

You may ask yourself: How can I be part of the changes? What weighs me down and keeps me from changing?

The Age of Changes will show us how to raise ourselves up and live with new vibrational energies. As we cling to older paradigms, the attraction to denser and lower levels of consciousness continues.

In reality, any Doomsday scenario is our own thought process that needs to be cleansed and purified. The end of the world does not necessarily mean the end of its life. Winter brings a significant change in nature with the promise of rebirth. The end refers to radical change in the present form of the world and how we are living. To access higher states of consciousness -- such as the Age of Aquarius is emanating – we need to prepare and train ourselves, step by step, in the skills necessary to catalyze transformation, transformation that will impact our society. We are entering a time of the Violet Flame, when violet vibrations will help us with our inner transformation as we connect to the heavenly realms.

The ultimate purpose of this change is to elevate us to our Divine Light Source.

To be part of the New Age and its changes, we must leave behind all frequencies that bring us down: fear, anger, resentment, past and present attachments, pain, etc. If we do not leave these low states behind and do not awaken to a new consciousness, we will not vibrate at higher frequencies and flow with our environment and the cosmos. Those who resist opening their mind and consciousness to rise above their ego will be subject to more pain and more tests; energetically, they will be exposed to continuous short circuits.

The universe is composed of Light, which holds scales of sounds and spectra of colors in a vast panoply of vibrations. Color and sound greatly influence our lives and our health.

The vibrations of the color violet correspond with the highest chakra. The seventh chakra is known as *Sahasrara*, located at the crown of the head. This energy point, or "chakra," is our connection to higher levels of Spirit, to multidimensional consciousness, and integrates all the chakras in our body. The opening of the crown chakra represents the culmination of the evolution of human awareness. Once liberated, our consciousness is able to easily enter into new realms of perception and knowing, moving beyond our limited mind and concepts. This chakra is ruled by the pineal gland and is the primary link between our soul and our brain, connecting us to multidimensional awareness.

Positive thoughts vibrate at a very high level and their colors are within the range of very fast frequencies; they are bright and clear, while our negative thoughts vibrate more slowly and their colors are denser, darker, duller, and opaque.

It is very important to understand that everything on planet Earth is experiencing changes in vibration. These in turn follow the trajectory of the flow of the vibrations of the universe.

Tune in to capture these vibrations of Love and Peace.

The "Schumann resonances" attempt to explain this phenomenon. German physicist W.O. Schumann stated in 1952 that the Earth is surrounded by a powerful electromagnetic field that is formed between the ground and the lower part of the ionosphere, situated some 100 km above us. This field possesses a more or less constant resonance (referred to as the Schumann resonance) of 7.83 pulses per second. From the 1980s to the present, however, it has increased to between 11 and 13 Hz.

And as this heartbeat of Mother Earth speeds up, time too is accelerating. These pulses function like a pacemaker and are responsible for the equilibrium of the biosphere, affecting all forms of life.

Our Positive vibrations within our thoughts, our words, and our actions help accelerate our growth toward higher consciousness.

It has been proven that all vertebrates and their brains are endowed with this same frequency of 7.83 Hz. It has been empirically observed that we cannot be healthy outside of this biologically natural frequency. When astronauts remain outside of the Schumann resonance during their extended space voyages, their bodies (bone density, in particular) are adversely affected. But when they are exposed to the action of a "Schumann simulator," they recover their equilibrium and health. For thousands of years Mother Earth's heartbeat has had a steady frequency of pulsations, and life has developed in relative, ecological equilibrium.

This resonance is our grounding energy connector to our "Mother"-Earth.

Currently, a similar situation is confronting those who do not express openness to higher levels. Their experiences throughout life are of a more primitive nature. They are living connected to low negative thoughts, words and actions; they are creating a constant electrical short- circuit in their lives.

As electromagnetic fields and resonances keep increasing, we also have to learn how to raise our own energy fields.

In the world of invisible energy vibration, human beings are no longer individuals or separate entities. In this dimension, they are part of *the Totality.*

If a high percentage of the population continues to vibrate at low levels, these massive changes will be met with great resistance and far less fluidity.

As a result, many of us are feeling impelled to be part of the ascent to higher states of consciousness. Willingness to refine our vibratory frequency, to live in harmony with the planet, and to move away from the actions that invite destruction will prepare us for the environmental changes and a balanced adjustment to the new reality.

Many of the children born today -- and some who were born in earlier times -- already possess a higher vibration in sync with the Age of Aquarius. Because of this association, they are called indigo children. *These children are said to have advanced souls and are born to help humanity in the process of change. They can be recognized by their great sense of responsibility, their highly developed intuition, and their affection for animals, the Earth, and the waters. They distance themselves from everything that is wasteful and aggressive, and they can connect to invisibility in a natural way.*

It is critical to observe objectively how our influence on our associates, and on the world in general, harms or helps. To be a beneficent presence in the world is an ideal goal.

The changes we realize within ourselves will be reflected in a better quality of life for all. Our inner being will demonstrate greater harmony and force for good. Those who vibrate in love and peace, rejecting fear as the director of their lives, will notice the transformation and will flow in harmony with experiences that generate universal changes.

Those who vibrate at low levels, controlled by fear and the shadows of the ego, will also reflect these realities with greater intensity.

You may have noticed that nowadays the color violet is used more and more frequently in garments and decorations. Without realizing it, we are already seeking out and following these vibrations. The world is evolving and demanding energetic changes. To realize these changes, people are creating events on a personal and global level that shake off negativity. They are cleansing themselves in order to heal and rise above the limitations of the material world.

We are learning to recognize our union with others and to know that the force lies in unity, not separation.

Emotions that are related to lesser levels, and are found beneath wounds that have apparently closed but have not yet healed, reappear in order to give individuals an opportunity to process and abandon them, and instead become Beings of Light.

Relationships that are based upon control and authority, attachment and emotional dependence, and have little to do with love; they will break and continue to die out. Those who lie, hurt, or commit acts of physical or mental cruelty will be punished for their actions. Their vibratory level will cause a short circuit, and their punishment will be immediate because the external vibrations will burn them.

Today I ask that you do the following: If you are attacked, don't respond. Forgive the individual who does not yet have the capacity to love and feel empathy and compassion and is trapped in lower levels of conciousness. By not forgiving, you continue to be connected to the person indefinitely.

If you don't forgive and you respond by attacking the aggressor, you will descend to his level. Aggressors during these times are destined to disappear. Don't lose your peace of mind and soul by submitting to any person or situation.

The spirit can't be humiliated, but the ego can.

These changes will stir the artist awakening within us. Those who are dissatisfied in their work will look for ways to be creative. This new awareness will stimulate the artistic, creative right side of the brain, breaking ties to the dense, material world and freeing us to move toward the lighter and brighter world of the imagination. The old paradigm will change completely.

If Gaia and the universe continue to speed up, our environment will vibrate faster every day. Humanity must be prepared to do the same. This is part of the change of 2012, and beyond. Every human being, plant, and animal contains and emanates energy of a specific vibration. Our mission must be to focus on learning to refine that frequency, which in turn depends on our level of consciousness.

To live in harmony, we must realize that the human body is becoming increasingly in tune with its internal energy. Balance between the physical material plane and the all-pervading Divine is also being realized.

Presently we are being exposed to energy changes that our body does not yet know how to process, resulting in headaches, more allergies, and various other symptoms that are more common today than ever before. Our sensibilities, including intuition, are becoming sharper.

Reflections

Self-assurance arises from knowing that we belong to a greater whole, and is diminished when we disregard others, and ourselves, in an unloving light. To regain trust and understanding of our essential identity is the foundation for the construction of a new humanity.

How much time will pass before we discover the Divinity in the depths of every human being? Before we see ourselves as magnificent creatures, playing an essential and indispensable role in Creation?

We are drops of water in a vast ocean, and tiny sparks of the Light of the Creator.

Most people fear radical changes, and just about everyone fears endings. That's because being attached to anything always includes the fear of losing it. When we lose faith, we invite uncertainty into our lives.

It helps to be aware that all our thoughts and feelings emit signals through invisible colors and sounds. These signals are picked up by other people and are heard throughout the universe. This energy naturally attracts similar energies, and that is how we attract to our lives the people and experiences that fulfill our expectations.

To not flow with the incoming vibrations is to be living at a lower level. As we open to fuller consciousness, it is essential that we act to liberate our creative forces. With creativity unleashed, we can co-create our lives in a masterful way. As I've said before, meditation and the Arts are very important in opening these sacred creative forces.

A thought creates the appearance of separation. But while it may seem that we are just individuals, separated from one another, the reality is that there is no separation at all. Whatever we do affects the whole world. Whether we do good or less than good, our doing ripples outward to the whole of humanity.

The fruit of our life is a personal responsibility.
We have the power to open our eyes (or to keep them closed)
and to awaken to the magnificent being that we
truly are, as we focus on Light and not on darkness.

Our body responds to all messages it receives...
Be scrupulously careful about the thoughts you let in to it.

There comes a time when we realize that there is no
separation from other human beings – or
from any form of life on Earth.
While our bodies are unique, our Light Source is the same.

I Am that I Am when I can see your Light as mine.

We can't exist as human beings in isolation. Discovering and
embracing our interconnectedness, we expand our life's
purpose by opening to love. Recognizing our innate nature
as love and our limitless power to love puts us in communion
with *the Supreme Love that animates all of humanity.*

The Supreme purpose of Life...
Is to discover Love.

From Love, Compassion is born.

My Notes:

_____

_____

_____

_____

From Heaven to Earth © 2009 Jacqueline Ripstein

Lesson XV

From Heaven to Earth

*"All men are by nature equal, made all of the same earth by one Workman;
and however we deceive ourselves,
as dear unto God is the poor peasant as the mighty prince." Plato*

*To be in "Heaven" means to have our consciousness vibrate at the
highest levels while we are in the physical dimension of life.*

*As the Light shines through, negativity will be shaken off more forcefully,
helping us to relinquish the dark vibrations that for centuries
have been activated by the shadows of the ego system.*

*NOW is our opportunity to reveal our Light.
Our Light is a sparkle of God's Light.*

*We may be confident of our own shining future and of freeing ourselves
from the trap of fears.*

*Our pursuit of human rights is part of a broad effort to use our great power
as we reveal the true Self that shines within all of us.*

*The Arts are our most powerful tool to break away from the boundaries of the mind;
imagination liberates us from all boundaries, showing us the path to the Light.
The Arts and our creative forces are the bridge to our Divine Being.
Our heart is connected to the Spirit world, while the mind chats through the ego.
Ego weakens us; Spirit strengthens us.
Our breath is our connection to Life.*

*Meditation and prayer carry us along the boundless road of awakening.
Meditation connects us to our Invisible power.*

*Gratitude and Compassion are the highest vibrations of Love.
Change starts with...Me, and with You.
Together we can all bring Heaven to Earth.*

*H*ow will you create a World of Peace and help manifest Love on this New Earth? Your role is unique and essential to help re-create a new world of wonderful changes. Are you ready? The New Consciousness, the Awakening, the Time of Light has begun! Welcome to a New Era!

Ego is the system of darkness, while Love is the instrument of the Light.

This is the ultimate lesson. This Key depicts the entry to your Divine Self. This lesson encompasses our life's journey as individuals, communities, and as One Humanity. It's the most fundamental of all life lessons -- to unite Heaven and Earth. This painting leads you on a spiritual journey through its high vibration, taking you ever deeper into the recesses of your inner Being. Its goal is to reconnect you to the Divine within you.

Now we discover the resources that help us embrace this beautiful new reality. Our journey is entirely about awakening; our days of vain voyaging are over. As you add meaning and purpose to your life, directing your thoughts, words, and actions toward the realization of life-enhancing goals, a life of light abundance will unfold for you.

Each lesson in this book has a purpose. The purpose is to awaken reunion with our Soul. As we polish ourselves as a diamond, we grow; we shine through our physical existence. Each lesson is a step to your awakening, a compilation of wisdom to support you to live your most empowered, fulfilled, abundant, and optimum life. Life is a school, a constant learning. All those who come into your life are meant to be your teachers. Every soul enables the opportunity to mirror you.

The English word spirit comes from the Latin "spiritus", meaning "breath," but also "spirit, soul, courage, vigor," revealing to us that within the breath is hidden the route to the truth of who we truly are. Take a deep breath, and let's journey together into a world of Love and Peace, a world where we teach our children to be free, happy as they manifest their Divine Light!

From the beginning of your life, the conditions you required for your learning were blueprinted. The lessons have shown you that only you are responsible for what you choose and for all actions you take. You then start your path through the grades of school...learning, floundering, falling, and standing up again. All experiences we have are here to help us grow as we cross over all barriers that fears and the ego create. To complete this life's journey is to have incorporated the learning and awakened the consciousness, as we see the Creator within us in every moving atom, in all people, animals, plants, stones, and in all creation.

During this time of transition, we realize how our souls connect, and we find we may nurture self-love and love of others. Awakening to our soul, we unveil our eternal unity with God. Hope and Faith give joyous sparkle to our lives, even in a world where everything seems to quickly go stale. As we learn how to dig deep within ourselves, we will find the strength to overcome and succeed in any situation we deal with.

The only battle to be won is to conquer ourselves first.

It is up to us to confront the truth of our reality: either we awaken and begin to make small changes to help rebuild our world, or we sit down, do nothing, and let chaos take over our humanity. You decide.

The purpose of this lesson is to broaden your perspective, to help you see your Oneness with all of creation. Deepening your commitment to planetary life, you will help to build a healthy, peaceful world that we will bequeath to future generations. Expansion of Consciousness must inevitably express itself as a blissful state of Peace on Earth.

The Mayan calendar clearly suggested that we entered a new kind of era. Other traditions—Hindu, Buddhist, Incan, Hopi, and others -- have also prophesied about these great changes. Kabbalah teaches us that we are already entering an awaited eternal time -- the time of the Messiah.

From Heaven to Earth © 2009 Jacqueline Ripstein

Same painting seen under Black Light.
Invisible Art and Light Technique © Pat

The vibrations continue accelerating as we enter a new Era of Light.

A New Age, an Era of Gold... a New Renaissance, the Rebirth of Humanity is happening right now.

In this modern-day Renaissance, the Arts, spurred by the creative forces and the imagination, will be necessary to help us evolve and adapt to the new conception of human beings and the world. When we awaken to our spirituality, we will restore a world of Peace, Love, Faith, and freedom, both within and outside of ourselves.

Our civilization is enduring drastic changes. These changes propel us with ever greater force and speed so that individually and collectively we may discover our true essence. Every era brings the kind of change needed to achieve the inevitable evolution.

Some of the changes we are living through today arise from the extreme materialism that our civilization has fallen into. The true identity of our Spiritual Being is starting to shine through the veils of matter and will be revealed as the light pierces through these veils.

The search for truth is a road of self-discovery.

Ask yourself: Have I maximized my potential? Before you sell yourself short, know that you can expand and grow as you lift the veils of darkness. If you are reading these words, it means you have ignited the courage to change and rise to a higher level of life.

With the vibrations being so high nowadays, it is necessary to learn to protect ourselves by moving away from the daily stress and chaos of low emotional vibrations, negative influences, and mundane, superfluous living. The term Ascension will be used to describe the transformation of the human being. This new transformation may also be seen as a metamorphosis; we have been in our cocoons for too long. Our time has come to emerge and spread our wings as the true Light beings that we are...and to fly! The Ascension process requires self-mastery in order to merge the thinking physical being – that lives inside the material and physical world -- with the Spiritual Being that lives within us and uses the body as its instrument to achieve growth through everyday life experiences. The Universe conspires to help us with this rebirth since everything in it --the Milky Way (and unimaginably beyond it) -- moves and takes up positions that contribute to making this happen. The Universe is aware that we need a safe and healthy world in which to fully express our own creativity.

Self-Mastery begins with our letting go of the past, learning to live in the Present moment where life is taking place, and letting go of our fears; as we do so, we become lighter. To be aware of the ego's function is a necessary element in the discovery of our Light. The second step is the awareness that all tests and storms we encounter are here to help us grow, to chip away our dark spots, and to teach us to be *the Architects of our Own Destiny.* As we learn and become aware, our states of consciousness rise; we become aware that we are the Soul, and that the Soul is the energy that gives life to the physical body, which is but our earthly vehicle. The third step is about the thought, mastering our thoughts, and allowing only those that we prefer. Doing so takes us to our next step, which has to do with our words. We start to think twice before we release our words, for once they are spoken, the energy comes out of our body to manifest. The last step in this awareness process is to take responsibility for our actions.

The inspirational vibrations of this painting guide us through the world shifts we are now experiencing – the entry to the heavens is now an opened door; the challenges and opportunities we are facing are here to help us rise to our magnificence.

It is said that those of us living through these changing times are blessed to experience the first rays of this so-called "Era of Light." As you are reading these words, know that your soul chose to be part of this unique transitional moment. Living through these changes imparts a great responsibility for us to wake up. United, we will create the new Renaissance of a safe and peaceful era for our children to inherit.

What is change? Is it a disaster or an opportunity?
Is it really the end of the world?

Change does not necessarily include a disaster. We live in unsettling times when what we believe we know, and think we control, has slipped from our hands. The premises on which humanity has based its beliefs are false -- they're mere illusion. Little by little, as the illusion falls apart, the truth that has been so elusive to humans will be apparent. The process is out of our hands; what is in our hands is to be and act with consciousness.

Each Era has had a correspondence to a certain color vibration, and within that color are multiple meanings that bear messages to help guide us. We are leaving behind the Age of Pisces, corresponding to the emanations of the color blue. Blue awakens our spirituality, nurturing us with its high-loving spiritual vibrations; it connects us to our creative powers and is the bridge between the physical body and the higher dimensions. As we enter the Age of Aquarius, the color violet -- which corresponds to the highest vibrations – is emanating most strongly. And we are receiving these intense waves of energy without realizing it. Violet color vibrations correspond to our highest portal of energy, the crown chakra. These vibrations illuminate our connection to the Divine Being, enlivening our imagination and spirituality. Violet hues assist those who seek the meaning of life and spiritual fulfillment, revealing our unity with Divine Consciousness through their high vibrations. The Violet Flame is an energy that helps us with transmutation; it empowers us to overcome low vibrations associated with fears and false beliefs. As we identify false identities and habit patterns, we can then tap into the Invisible World to find our truth.

From Heaven to Earth © 2009 Jacqueline Ripstein
Same painting seen under Normal & Black Lights.
Invisible Art and Light Technique © Pat

These new energies are activating our DNA and therefore our consciousness, and are accelerating our metamorphosis. "Downloaded" from a greater
source, these energies may be likened to upgrades to "higher voltages" within
all of life. By activating our energy field of light, our Spirit becomes stronger
and more active, and stands out over material things. Our intuition is sharp-
ened, our creativity stimulated. Our need to connect with these higher forces
intensifies daily. Meditation, the arts, prayer, compassion, and forgiveness are
invaluable in this process of cleansing negativity and inspiring our human
growth.

The "Breath of Life" happens within the space between one breath and another, and it is here where one discovers the "zero point" where all creation
happens. It is within the invisible realms that all life is created and manifested.
It is where everything comes from, and where the Spirit and the Creator merge.
It is the cradle of infinite Love, Light, and Peace.

Scientists say that the magnetic field from the Sun is more than 230
percent stronger than it was at the beginning of the twentieth century
(1901). Its global energetic activity has been growing steadily, creating
an excitation of activity that directly influences us -- our physical body
as much as our emotional and spiritual body. It is affecting everything
relative to all life on the planet. Many scientists, including Dr. Alexey
Dmitriev, are seeing that the moon is growing in atmosphere, and that the
magnetic fields of the planets are getting stronger. Like these examples,
changes are occurring throughout the entire galaxy. These higher energy
field changes are affecting the Milky Way, and the whole universe is
responding to these changes, which are also affecting us, giving us the
opportunity to raise our own vibrations, activating our intuition, telepa-
thy, clairaudience, and clairvoyance. As the human mind is expanding
in its perceptive abilities, also the planet earth is dynamically altering

in its magnetic frequency. It is our inner work and the awareness of our thoughts that will create the ascension process. To clarify, 'energetic resonance' refers to an energy field of Planet Earth that has been accelerating in recent decades and is affecting both its own life and human evolution.

We are all feeling a personal change, making us realize that the world is different now than it was before. The energy is pushing us to rediscover our creative forces, our Light, to Unite. These forces are very necessary in moments of change. Those who have or who will develop "right-brain" qualities, such as creativity, inventiveness, empathy, and compassion, will lead us throughout this era more. Our left brain is our analytic brain -- it connects us to the material world -- while our right brain is our direct connection to our passion, our creative forces, our inner emotions, to our Spiritual Being. Our intuition will be our ally once again, since it is through intuition that we will begin to discern the road ahead.

The left-brain is about control;
the right-brain is all about freedom and awareness.

It is an essential assignment in the School of Life that we pass through all kinds of experiences; they force us to grow and discover the truth within us that has always been waiting to be revealed.

From primitive times, when man led a rudimentary life, to the present time of breakthrough discoveries in science, technology, culture, and the arts, doors have been steadily opening to the deeper and more mysterious essence of life. We have waited for this moment, when what we have sought for so long is finally in the process of manifesting.

Everything in creation is perfect and contains the seed of consciousness within it. Through the communion of the four elements, every person, every animal, every living entity is contained within the other, and the existence of each one vibrates in the other.

Every kingdom vibrates with its own intensity—mineral, vegetable, animal, and human—and within each of us are the essences of the other kingdoms. Nothing is separate; everything is contained within everything else. Human beings have the unique opportunity to ascend to higher levels of consciousness. Each step towards ascension precipitates greater new insights, increased states of perception, and higher awareness. In the U.K. a group of prominent neuroscientists signed a proclamation called The Cambridge Declaration on Consciousness, acknowledging human and animal consciousness alike. (One of these scientists was Stephen Hawking.)

The use of creativity and imagination frees us from limited mind patterns. This privilege has a price: we have the responsibility to assist, maintain, preserve, and create balance, manifesting a world of Love and Peace. If the human being is in conflict, all the other kingdoms are affected by this conflict. Thus, when a kingdom falls out of balance, this causes a chain reaction in the others. Species of animals, plants, trees, and entire forests rapidly disappear, and contamination of lakes, rivers, oceans, and streams increases from the actions of human beings. We are experiencing the greatest wave of biological loss since the disappearance of the dinosaurs. When any species goes extinct, a part of us goes extinct with it.

We are at a very delicate tipping point in creation, a space where we either unite to help make the change, or leave the result in the hands of fate. By doing nothing we allow negative energies to take control. But there is still hope, thanks to the efforts of people aware of the crisis. Some governments and many foundations are now working on plans for action. People have begun to join forces to educate and take measures that can help avoid more catastrophes. We have two options: generate positive change or fall into a dark labyrinth with no future.

New educational programs for our children stress the interconnectedness of all and our responsibilities in honoring that unity. Our children are very advanced souls but they need to be guided to the truth of who they are as spiritual beings having a physical experience. Knowing who they are will ease the sense of separation, with all its stress and pressure. Mainly, we need to emphasize that peace -- not war, and cooperation -- not competition, is the answer.

Now we know that all damage we do outside of ourselves is creating the same damage within ourselves. Just a small example: we cut down a tree and we have less oxygen to breathe. Trees absorb carbon dioxide, a significant contributor to global warming – it is estimated that a single tree can remove a ton of CO_2 per day. Trees evaporate water and release moisture through their leaves; tree roots stabilize soil and prevent erosion; trees filter rainwater; they provide shelter and home for many kinds of animal species and plants; their leaves trap dust and other harmful particles. As you can see, killing a single tree affects everything enormously. Just imagine what killing a forest can do! Do you think it's a coincidence that our respiratory system is similar to trees and branches upside down? It's even called "The Bronchial Tree."

Every bomb that explodes, and every bullet that's fired, and every invective that is uttered creates a massive vibration that resonates throughout the Earth in search of a way out. The vibration is liberated by means of tremors, earthquakes, floods, tsunamis, and other natural disasters that can occur anywhere. Everything has a price in life--every action has a reaction.

We have discovered how to fly and how to descend to the bottom of the oceans. We have conquered the tallest mountain, gone into space, created a digital world, analyzed the most remote cells in the body -- and discovered that all is energy. But I ask myself, have we discovered the Being of Light that longs to be found and that lies within each of us? Can we see beyond darkness?

A New humanity will come forth as the World of Illusion collapses!

Civilizations have borne witness to great confrontation between the forces of Light and the forces of darkness. Our modern civilization is at the peak of this confrontation. The ego revolts with the greatest force when faced with the threat of its extinction in the Light. This confrontation between the forces of darkness and Light is active not only outside of us, but inside of us as well.

While the Light invites us to wake up, the ego hides us in the material world of illusion. It praises us and anesthetizes us so we don't abandon it; it keeps us busy and in perpetual stress. It amplifies noise and distractions to keep us from "finding time" to meditate in silence and take steps toward creative freedom. The ego and its dark vibration have kept everything under control.

As the Light shows its grandeur, the ego system begins to wobble.
Through our focus on the Light, ego is increasingly weakened.
Gratitude elevates us.
One by one, we drop the masks that presented our false face.

How we identify ourselves and where our thoughts are determines our level of consciousness. Living focused only in this material world, our awareness stays finite. As we break from the ego's illusion boundaries, the Invisible and Infinite World will then start to reveal itself to us!

Thoughts of limitation and negation of any kind are pollutants also.
We are constantly bombarded by thoughts from within and without.

By not being aware of our own thoughts and how to control them,
the turnaround is that they end up bombarding and controlling us.

The breath helps us outflow stress
and contain any bombardment of thoughts.

We are now witnessing the dawn of a new recognition of the Light! We are living a unique time, where more knowledge and empowerment are being released now, with less control. From our birth moment, we are conditioned to what is "right and wrong," "good and bad." With the Light comes a new recognition that involves a state of self-awareness that moves us far away from all limitations, into the awareness of a greater understanding of the Oneness of all Life.

Art for me is a tool to be present in a pure state of Awareness.

Creativity is a form of energy consciousness and it manifests in different ways. It's based in a subconscious level; as we increase awareness, our creativity rises to conscious levels.

By using our creative ability, we can create in a given moment any experience we visualize. The key issue is not to be scattered, but rather to focus to create it.

It took me five years to finish the painting of this lesson. During this time, I experienced various processes: deaths, losses, and illnesses that made me realize many things. Being unable to express myself after these tragedies crippled my speech, and with my vital energy depleted, I nonetheless found the strength to overcome these trials and to write this book, which the Spirit was dictating to me. Each painting has taught me a different secret about life which I'd never unveiled completely; only what I used to call "the essences" of each piece were displayed for years in my art.

I was guided by messages given to me by my "teachers," who told me thirty years ago that my mission was to assist in the Ascension from Earth to Heaven. With this painting I understood that my mission had finally begun, and that it was being activated and encouraged.

The painting presented in this lesson revealed to me that human beings have the capacity to raise themselves from the Earth toward Heaven. We are physically made of Earth elements, and what gives the body life and energy is made of the Divine Spirit that dwells within each of us. I discovered that to elevate ourselves to Heaven we must have our feet firmly rooted in the physical world, with the conscious understanding that the material world is merely clothing. The physical world is merely a vehicle. Whoever moves beyond the vehicle and continues to express, as the Light within is able to rise to the Creator.

The difference between being on the Earth or in Heaven is the multiple levels of vibration between these two states of consciousness. From the sleep-like state, the lower depressed levels where one falls victim to numbness, lethargy, and confusion, one may rise to the most sublime and ineffable states of awareness. One level of consciousness segues to the next. The ego influences these states of consciousness, marking the difference between a human being who "thinks" and believes him- or herself to be "special," and the more humble person who is aware that all beings are equally worthy. Love is also indicative of our "level" of wakefulness in life. Love may progress from genuine self-love to love of others and all that is alive, including animals, trees, and whatever appears before our eyes. Love in its selfless state expresses as un-self-conscious service and natural empathy and compassion for others, the highest form of love.

Enlightenment knows no bounds. It's a never-ending path.

Our perception of time is changing in relation to certain aspects of daily life. As the Schumann frequencies speed up, time also speeds up, along with the vibratory frequencies of Planet Earth and the Universe. Time is offering a new experience; we need to learn to use our time more wisely and not waste other people's time! We need to identify and work on our vanity so that our time may be filled not with paeans of praise to ourselves and bids for attention, but with joy and happiness that we share with others.

Choose your "battles" wisely. Nowadays, we can deal with challenges from a higher level. Look for these solutions.

Don't engage in someone else's anger or battles; don't give away your Peace.

It's important to understand the relationship between time, vibration, and consciousness. All are interrelated. Our consciousness emits vibratory frequencies that progress through various levels. Only by being present in the present moment can consciousness be ignited. Higher Consciousness leads to very fast frequencies that manifest a wakeful state, wherein we connect and emanate all vibrations. Those that are revealed to us -- joy, love, compassion, service, and peace -- can only be of higher levels.

The lower consciousness drags along in low and slow vibratory dimensions created by low-level thoughts and emotions that produce fear, pain, depression, anger, pride, guilt and self-pity. Guilt is an excuse to sabotage our lives. Anger and revenge create an ego- state wherein human beings think and act primitively, without taking responsibility for the pain they inflict upon themselves and others. The rigid pride of ego sees to it that blindness prevails, identifying the "other" person and situation to always be at fault – never oneself. In this very low state, humans become the "victims" of all unfavorable circumstances. It's always startling when we catch ourselves giving away our inner power to people and adverse circumstances!

Pain generates anger and anger generates hatred. They are all entangled. When we release one, the other can also be freed.

The new frequencies give us the opportunity to climb higher. The Universe utilizes all of its instruments to achieve its Ascension.

When we crash emotionally, a revelation takes place, as it exposes our delusions and unmasks the ego system that has nourished those illusions. False identity is then exposed.

Fed by the ego, suffering returns to us endlessly, insatiably seeking to make us addicted to it. Do we deserve to be happy, prosperous, healthy, and successful? Of course we do! And to realize this harmony, we need to learn to break away from the ego's traps.

Resistance holds us back and creates even more resistance and pain. Resisting illness does not permit change or healing; rather, it generates deeper levels of illness. Despair and suffering, as well as depression, express as chronic symptoms in humans. These symptoms are stored by "Morphic fields" (*1). When we are drawn to lower energetic fields of suffering, our energetic antennas attune to the suffering in these fields, which we then manifest more deeply, appropriating them as our own. As I see it, "Morphic fields" or "information fields" are electromagnetic spaces wherein all information is "stored." They are energetic fields that link all beings, influencing the learning and habits of all people and all life. New knowledge and inventions create new fields of awareness, which gain strength as others pick up this awareness. I see it as the space or field where all computers "store their memories." It is a never-ending space where a lot of knowledge is stored. I believe that artists like Leonardo da Vinci have been able to "download" information that was "stored" in these fields of infinite consciousness.

What must we do to flow with the changes, and ascend? Be awake and aware—not asleep or lethargic. We must control our thoughts and look inside ourselves to be able to discern the true reality on the outside.

(*1) Rupert Sheldrake, on Morphic Fields:

"Morphic field" is a term introduced by Sheldrake. He proposes that there is a field within and around a "morphic unit" which organizes its characteristic structure and pattern of activity. [19] According to Sheldrake, the morphic field underlies the formation and behavior of "holons" and "morphic units," and can be set up by the repetition of similar acts or thoughts. The hypothesis is that a particular form belonging to a certain group, which has already established its (collective) morphic field, will tune into that morphic field. The particular form will read the collective information through the process of "morphic resonance," using it to guide its own development. This development of the particular form will then provide, again through morphic resonance, feedback to the morphic field of that group, thus strengthening it with its own experience, resulting in new information being added (i.e., stored in the database). Sheldrake regards the morphic fields as a universal database for both organic (genetic) and abstract (mental) forms.

Human beings possess an enormous capacity for overcoming difficulties. The learning acquired through mistakes is the beginning of a new individual and collective stage of growth. The desire to learn allows us to ascend rapidly, to live and flow without resistance in the face of the changes we are experiencing. .(http://en.wikipedia.org/wiki/Rupert_Sheldrake.)

Thinking in a positive and unguarded way is indispensable, since this is how we create high vibrations of energy that provide the impulse to ascend. Low actions and thoughts take us downward.

We must accept that we are united with everything and that we contain everything— in infinite consciousness. To create is to be part of a "conscious evolution" toward the New Age of Light and Peace.

What kind of world do you want to leave for your children and their progeny?

We are at a turning point where each of us must participate in restoring and preserving all life on Planet Earth. Any great evolutionary shift requires the fires of refinement, as it's in the burning away of dross that new life emerges. We are the beneficiaries of great lessons and ages-old wisdom, warning us not to repeat the same old mistakes. All who are alive today and choose to be part of these radical changes have the unique opportunity to help build the foundation for new growth. The time has come for opening our eyes to new possibilities, new imaginings, and the opportunity to create joyful change in the years ahead.

Our children need our help; they have become confused, following a pattern of anger, wars, hatred, and separation. They have learned to injure each other and imitate our acts of war between them. The games of war are affecting their own peace of mind.

Humbly, we must all ask for forgiveness from Planet Earth and all of life. Be grateful every day for the multiple blessings we are given and for the great tests that have made us grow as individuals and as a society.

As we wake up, one by one, we will know that Heaven is inside of us and that we are connected to every being that vibrates in this sacred and invisible space.

Our external fighting shows us that we are still at war with ourselves. The day is coming, however, when instead of judging and pointing fingers at others and ourselves, we will see clearly, compassionately, and constructively. We will gain the strength and consciousness that effect changes in ourselves. We will see that in the end, everything we experience is a projection and reflection of our inner state, and that the real confrontation --- which involves no "fighting" at all -- is with ourselves, with our own ego. When we stop creating inner wars, outer wars will cease.

As we awaken, we master ourselves.

Opening consciousness means taking responsibility for all our actions and rethinking their effects on the world. Consciousness has multiple levels, which go hand in hand with our spiritual growth.

A Oneness prayer: *We send Light and Love with our prayers to all human beings who are suffering—those who seem trapped by their fears and hopelessness, those who don't know love or are afraid to love, those who lack inner strength. We send Light and gratitude to Mother Earth, to her elements and to all of life on this planet that sustains us. To the extinct beings, we ask forgiveness for not being able to help save them, and we give them thanks for having existed.*

Forgiveness is the most liberating energy that exists. For my part, I forgive everyone who has hurt me along my way, whether with a weapon or a word. I forgive all those of evil tongue and hateful words, for truly, by lacking the consciousness of higher levels, they "know not what they do." I have forgiven myself and I ask for forgiveness from those I have hurt.

As we keep our vision and energy in the Light, we focus on generating more Light and Love.

Reflections

A New Era has dawned; now it is up to us to take responsibility and to act in the interests of all. *The uplifting vibrations of this painting guide us through the world shifts we are now experiencing -- the challenges and opportunities we are facing individually as well as collectively.*

What is New Earth Consciousness? It describes the shift from a fearful pain-based model of living to a higher one, based on love, compassion, and consciousness. The energy of this New Consciousness is shifting how the planetary system works, defining a new pattern in the harmonics of the DNA of all life. It is time for expansion, for evolvement, a time to expand our thoughts into higher positive realms of creation. It is our time to shine!

Now! ... is our opportunity to liberate our lives from the limitations of the ego's material world.

Consciousness is defined as: "being aware of one's existence, sensations, thoughts, emotions, and surroundings." "Intelligence is the capacity to learn.

Animals live present to their lives; we humans move as tidal waves between the past and the future, losing the momentum of *our Presence in the present moment of Life.*

The chopping down of trees is analogous to our slicing off the branches of our bronchial system. The destruction of each tree diminishes the quality and quantity of oxygen and, as a result, allergies and other illnesses increase.

Understand that change is happening on multiple levels: humanity, all living entities, the planet itself, the Milky Way, the Universe; indeed, all of creation is participating in a simultaneous leap in evolution wherein the Light is being revealed from more advanced dimensions. New portals are opening.

The "wise" person assists the world by being aware and responsible in his words, thoughts, and actions, knowing that everything he does impacts all of Creation. He or she is a beneficent presence in the world.

Ascension of our lives is a personal responsibility that affects all of humanity. It demands that we give it time and our complete attention. Through our positive decisions and actions, we realize change and elevate the world in which we live. We ascend to Heaven by being more aware. Love unites us with higher dimensions, as Heaven descends to receive us with Love.

The realization of the perfection which is already within me recognizes: "The Father who abides in me, He does the work." In other words, He is the Source...within me..."I Am that I Am."

We must set an example for future generations -- our children imitate us. They need to see our love and hope in action, to be encouraged in their creativity and their meditation, and to experience more moments of Peace.

As we join to create a new model for holistic living, our focus is ever on restoring Hope, focusing on our Light and not on darkness. We will breathe pure air, appreciating life every morning; we will listen to the song of birds and smell the roses. These are not poetic flights of fancy but the small things and acts that delight us and give us hope.

It is essential to see the positive side of life and focus on it. It is just as essential to see the negative side of life without fear or resistance – see it clearly and then let it go. Be thankful for what you have, and don't focus on what you do not have.

Focusing on wants and needs holds us in that energy of want and need, limiting the Universe from giving us more abundance.

Ascension will come about as harmony is realized within each human being, and as we reestablish our intimate and loving relationship with the environment. Ascension is the union of the human Spirit with the Spirit of the Creator.

Heaven is seen in everything that is alive and vibrating in the highest spheres of Creation.

The Earth is a platform on which this truth may be experienced. Maya, or the World of Illusion, will slowly crumble, as little by little the Invisible World -- where we find our true reality-- is revealed.

"Fall seven times, stand up eight." Japanese Proverb.

The Dawning of a New World and a New You has reached a crescendo.
The more we focus in the Light as One Humanity, the more the forces of darkness, of the ego system, will crumble.

New Earth Consciousness arises as the result of Awareness, which may often be strengthened by Silence, Prayer, and Meditation. The Arts are tools to help us realize and express our Divine Unity.

Active creativity and the imagination are among the most glorious and beautiful portals to the realization of Oneness.
It is for us to know it, love it, be it.

Birth and Death are not a choice...Heaven on Earth ...is a choice!
The Greek sages once said: Foolish are those who live beneath the stars; wise are those who rise above them. Know that you may rise above all limitations of your mind; graciously accept your Inner Power and shine your Light.

If you don't control your thoughts, actions, and mind,
someone else will be all too happy to do it.

External brute force is weakness; internal force is our real strength.
Each breath we take is an opportunity to connect to Spirit.

As we reveal our Soul and our Light, the Invisible World will become visible.
I encourage you to participate in these times of changes so that you may discover and manifest this unprecedented journey of your own Spirit and that of all humankind.

Your loving participation will help create a World of Peace and Love for our children and their children.
When love manifests as Unconditional Love,
a force greater than yourself sparkles.
Let your life be your message to the world.

My Notes:

_____

_____

_____

_____

Jacqueline Ripstein

Fine Art Artist, Author & Healing Pioneer, creator of the Invisible Art Technique.
World Peace Envoy
United Nations ECOSOC Representative for the International Association
of Educators for World Peace.

"Only those who see the Invisible can do the Impossible"....JR©™

Internationally renowned artist Jacqueline Ripstein has inspired thousands of people all over the world through her highly vibrational art, books, self-awareness seminars and workshops. Born in Mexico and self-taught, Jacqueline won a national diploma at age 12 in a Prismacolor competition. Featured at more than 375 international art shows, she's participated in major world gatherings where she received special honors some events are: Chosen to open the "Sefarad"events, in Toledo, Spain (1992-'94) Invited by the government; commissioned to paint Our Lady of the Universe for Medjugorje, Croatia, to support widows and orphans of war (1996); chosen to open the "Millennium Peace Day" in 2000 at the UN in NY, alongside Mrs. Nane Annan; leading a workshop for over 450 children, encouraging their messages of Peace to the World; invited by the government of China to celebrate the 9/21/2012 International Day of Peace; participation in the first Linzhou Art Exhibition and a Gliding Opening Gala at the Taihang Canyon Peach Blossom Valley, including a Ceremony of Friendship and Peace, with more than 3500 people in attendance, where Jacqueline was asked to be one of the representatives to close the ceremony using the peace water and bells. Jacqueline was also among the key speakers at the International Friendship Peace Forum, delivering a "Proposal to Use the Arts as an Instrument for World Peace."Some of her paintings have found a permanent home at the Museum of Characters in Linzhou, Henan Province, China. Invited to Hyderabad, India, where her art was chosen as the backdrop for the event, she was one of the keynote speakers at the First Parliament on Spirituality, in December 21, 2012.

A unique creative, that has dared cross the boundaries of the traditional art schools, to create new techniques in the world of art, Jacqueline's mystical journey and insatiable search for the Divine Light guided her to patent since 1986 the Invisible Art & Light Technique, a gift to humanity, a unique revelation, an encounter with our spiritual world through her art. Scientific research by Dr. Valerie Hunt,

Dr. J. J. Hurtak, Dr. Rafael López Guerrero, and Dr. Vaughn Cook, has revealed that her art has unique healing properties, and that it can elevate us to heightened states of consciousness.(See studies at http://www.jacquelineripstein.com.) Testimonials speak of how her art has changed and inspired the lives of thousands of people.

Praised by international art critics and collectors, Jacqueline has been working in collaboration with the UN to reach its Eight Millennium Development Goals. Jacqueline has dedicated her life to helping raise human consciousness through her art, as well as motivational and self-awareness books, seminars, and workshops. An advocate for peace, she champions the arts and the creative forces as instruments for world peace.

"My goal in creating New Invisible Art Techniques has been to reveal these unseen dimensions and to offer a breath of hope to our humanity by showing from where we create our lives, as the inner Light beings that we truly are. "I have realized that my art becomes a doorway, a portal to Invisible realms, connecting the viewer to emotional healing and spiritual power." To inspire people and help make a difference in their lives is my breath of Life."

Eternal Love seen under Normal Light.   *Same painting seen under Black Light.*   *Same painting seen under Normal & Black Lights.*

Homage to Rodin: *Eternal Love (1997)© with the patented Invisible Art & Light Technique by Jacqueline Ripstein (1986). You can view the same painting under three lights, Normal, Black Light and Both Lights.*

www.Jacquelineripstein.com
www.theartofhealingart.com

Made in the USA
San Bernardino, CA
08 January 2016